The Power In You

Also by Rachaele Hambleton

The Patchwork Family: Toddlers,
Teenagers and Everything in Between

Part-Time Working Mummy: A Patchwork Life

A Different Kind of Happy

The Power In You

How to Live and Love Your Life

RACHAELE HAMBLETON

ROBINSON

ROBINSON

First published in Great Britain in 2024 by Robinson

3 5 7 9 10 8 6 4 2

Copyright © Rachaele Hambleton, 2024
All illustrations from Shutterstock

The moral right of the author has been asserted.

A CIP catalogue record for this book
is available from the British Library.

ISBN: 978-1-47214-921-3

Typeset in Garamond by Hewer Text UK Ltd, Edinburgh
Printed and bound in Great Britain by Clays Ltd, Elcograf S.p.A.

Papers used by Robinson are from well-managed
forests and other responsible sources.

MIX
Paper | Supporting
responsible forestry
FSC
www.fsc.org   FSC® C104740

Robinson
An imprint of
Little, Brown Book Group
Carmelite House
50 Victoria Embankment
London EC4Y 0DZ

An Hachette UK Company
www.hachette.co.uk

www.littlebrown.co.uk

To me, aged four.
You've got this.

Contents

Prologue: A letter to my younger self, aged four (the morning after my mum left home)

Hey Baby Girl,

This, without doubt, is one of the most difficult letters I am ever going to write, and it breaks my heart even more that you have to read it. It's hard for me to explain things to you in a way you will understand, because you are so tiny, innocent and precious. I'm a grown-up now, raising a little boy the exact same age that you are now, writing this letter to you, and it still doesn't make much sense.

Darling girl, life has changed for you since yesterday. For the past (almost) five years, all you have known is your mummy. She is the one person you've spent every single day with. She is the one who loves you to the moon and back. She is the one who sings to you in the bath and strokes your cheek as you fall asleep every night. She has magical hands that stitch and sew to create lampshades that look like hot air balloons, and she makes bedspreads to match. She loses days in the garden potting the most beautiful flowers, and she looks forward to waking you up each day.

Your mummy is not here anymore. She's gone. There are reasons for this that you are too little to understand, but what you need to know is that she isn't coming back.

When you get out of bed this morning and go downstairs, your daddy will be there. He's never normally there; he's always at work. Usually it's just you and Mummy, and your brothers and sister until they go off to school and work, but today will be different. Your daddy will be sad when you see him. You've never seen him sad before. It's only Mummy who you've seen looking sad. He's going to be holding the black-and-white wedding picture of your mummy and him together. He'll be sitting on the floor at the bottom of the stairs, and he'll be crying. He won't hear you ask him why he's crying, and he won't answer you when you ask where your mummy has gone. One of your brothers is sad too, and your sister is angry, so don't go to them. Look for your eldest brother. He will try and explain things to you, and help you feel better when you're sad.

I want to tell you that you won't be sad for long, I want to tell you that things get will better, but they won't. Not for a while, anyway.

Everything has changed since yesterday, which you will notice straight away. You will feel different when you go to school, because you will notice you are the only little girl in your class who doesn't have a mummy. You will feel different every day to come, for many reasons. You will notice your friends' mummies kiss and hug them when they drop them off and pick them up, and you will feel a pain inside your body which is like a tummy ache, but in your heart. That pain will be there for a long time, but I promise that when you grow up, you will see that this all happened for a reason, and incredible things will come from these feelings. Trust me on that – and read this part of this letter again, over and over, when you feel that pain.

Within the next three weeks, your daddy is going to move the lady over the road into your home, along with her children. You know the lady I mean: Mummy doesn't like her, and she sounds like the milk lady when she whistles. You will share a room with her daughter, and that lady will sleep in bed with your daddy, where your mummy used to sleep. Daddy will keep working away, and she will look after you like your mummy did. But it won't be the same anymore, angel.

All the safe adults around you, other than your brother, will disappear along with your mummy. I want to tell you to be strong, to find your voice, to speak up and tell the truth, but you're too tiny to do that, and it's too much to ask of you, so instead I'm going to make you some promises. I hope they will keep you going on all the hard and bad days:

- You ARE going to be OK.
- You have ten years' worth of what's about to come. That sounds like a long time, but there will be days when you look back and think that it has all gone quite quickly.
- When you grow up, you will be surrounded by so much love. Love just like your mummy gave you. The kind where you fall asleep on the sofa in the afternoon, snuggled into someone who feels safe. One day you will become a mummy yourself, and your babies will love you so much it will make your heart happy – as happy as you were when you were with your mummy.

When you become an adult, you will understand how important it is to show emotions, and you will encourage everyone around you to feel their feelings – which is why what I am about to say hurts my heart. For the next ten years, you need to try and forget the first five ever happened so that you can survive. You're in self-preservation mode, and there are certain things you will have to do.

- Try not to show you're sad or upset. Try really hard to only get upset in front of your biggest brother. He's safe. You need to learn really quickly who's safe and who isn't.
- There are no hugs and kisses anymore, but remember that will all come back when you grow up and have your own babies.

♥ Try and be invisible at home, even with your daddy. The lady across the road doesn't like it when your daddy hugs you.

When you grow up, you will remember the good parts of the time you spent with your mummy. You'll remember the way she let you roller-skate round the house and the lunches she made you; you'll remember her voice, her thick Mancunian accent. And when your heart feels like it's snapping in two, you'll remember her smell. That sweet perfume on her soft, warm neck as you fell asleep snuggled into her every single afternoon while watching *Annie* on repeat.

But for right now, and for the next decade, just hang on in there. Things will get better. Things WILL come good again. You WILL feel love again, just like you did before your mummy left.

Don't give up, don't give in and don't answer back. Think of it as a game – a really rubbish one you won't enjoy, but one you will win in the end.

I'm watching over you. I love you. I am so proud of how strong you are about to be – and I will speak to you when we get there . . .

So many hugs,

Big, grown-up Rach xx

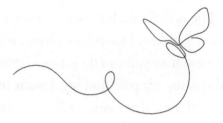

Introduction

I'm writing this book at a cute desk I chose, on a laptop I paid for, listening to my two dogs snore beside me. Usher is giving it beans over our Alexa, the fire is roaring, and my typing is only interrupted when I pause to dip a chocolate digestive into my cup of tea.

I feel like I've won the lottery. After all that I've seen and experienced in my lifetime, the lessons I've had to learn, this, right now, sitting here, living this life, this is what I have always hoped for. I feel lucky, but I also know I have made this my reality, step by step, challenge by challenge, year by year. I have learned to feel my own power and build my self-belief; I have had to trust that things would get better. I realised I could overcome the hand I had been dealt and make a life for myself – and for any other people who came along and needed me.

And it's those challenges and lessons that have made me want to write this book, to share my experiences so you feel less alone. If I can lose everything but still find peace, so can you. Life is difficult, but there is always hope. This book will show you how I found my power, my voice and my strength, and how you can do it too. Through sharing my ups and downs, my pain and joy, I want to show you how you can fill your days with sunlight, overcome your struggles and find your own way to live and be happier. We can all do it. That little-girl me, lost and scared without her mummy, might not have thought it was possible – but she did it.

My first (and worst) lesson

It was a Thursday when my mum left. A Thursday in late January in the 1980s. I don't remember much about that day. I have tried to find out what the weather was doing that day by searching online, just so I can try to picture it: was it raining, icy, or dry and cold? I can't find out, and I cannot remember. I do remember seeing my older sister crying in her room when I woke up. She was sitting on the end of her bed with her back to me. She had a long ginger spiral perm, and she was wearing a green pyjama top. I can still picture that like it was yesterday. I backed out of her room before she noticed me, and then I walked downstairs to my dad. He was sitting at the bottom of the stairs under this mahogany mirror we had; I remember it had lots of little shelves and different-sized mirrors on it, and it reminded me of a castle. My mum used to polish it all the time so the mirrors sparkled and the dark wood gleamed. He was sitting with his back against the wall, his feet straight out in front of him, crossed at the ankles. He had no socks on, and I remember looking at his toes. They flicked upwards, just like mine; just like my sister's. It was the first time I noticed we had something that looked the same. He was holding one of the wedding photos of him and my mum. It was black and white. He was holding it with both hands, and he was crying.

That's all I remember about that day. It would have been a school day, but I don't remember if my siblings or I went to school or work. I don't remember who told me our mum had left. I don't remember what I ate, what toys I played with, if I played at all. I don't remember if I watched *Annie* that day as normal, and I don't remember who put me to bed that night, or the night after, which seems odd considering it would have been such a huge thing, having been woken up and put to bed by my mum every night of my life before that. A few weeks later, on Valentine's Day, our neighbour moved in and our lives were turned upside down and back to front again.

We went from being a pretty normal, happy family, with no money worries and a beautiful home full of love, to the total opposite within a month. I was told by the neighbour that my mum didn't want me or love me. And instead of making things better, my dad just moved the neighbour and her kids into our home while he continued to go to work, often staying away from Sunday to Friday. We became her responsibility. A stranger's responsibility – within less than a month of losing our mum and all we'd ever known. My eldest brother and sister left home shortly after my mum did and I went from seeing my siblings every day to every few weeks and my mum only every few months.

This made me realise we were never a normal, happy family. Families full of love don't crumble as quickly as we did when one person leaves. I look back at pictures of us all in the 1970s and 1980s, some taken before I was born and others within the four and a half years since I had come along. They show us cockling on the beach, covered in mud, or posing on deckchairs at Pontins with huge smiles. And I wonder who we really were – as individuals and as a family. I also wonder how the Big Rach I am today would do things differently for her family to minimise the mess and heartbreak if something like this were to happen to us.

Possibly because of the lessons I've been learning since I was that little girl, I like to think that if my husband Josh or I were to make a decision that would tear our family apart, the other one would step up to make it better for the children, no matter how much pain we were all in. I struggle to see either of us ever repeatedly making decisions that could destroy our unit, and if one of us somehow did, I feel sure the other would harness their own power to make things better for everyone. I see now that I was not part of

a 'normal, happy family', because my parents both prioritised their own needs over those of their four children.
They witnessed our hearts snap in front of them, they
watched us all become shells of the children we once were,
and they still didn't change. They didn't stop and think,
'Fucking hell, my children need me right now.' When the
shit hit the fan, they both disappeared – and left us to
survive with the neighbour from over the road.

Using your past to heal you in the present

Writing things down has always been a great tool for me.
It's something I do every single day: making lists by hand,
typing notes into my phone, keeping a diary, journaling.
Putting pen to paper, whether physically or digitally, can
help us to work through our emotions, analyse them, and
work out how to learn from them and then move on.
Have you ever tried using writing as a tool for empower-
ment and growth? If not, I really recommend it.

One of the most effective examples of the power of
writing I've experienced was the time I made a timeline. I
can't remember where I got the idea from, but I noted the
dates of key incidents and memories on lots of little pieces
of paper, and then arranged them in chronological order,
placing them along a line, with the good things above the
line and the bad things below. The good things were minimal compared to the bad, but I still wanted to remember

them, as I felt it was important. Here, I've decided to share some of the best things that happened in the ten years I spent being cared for by the neighbour over the road.

1. She had a daughter who was five months younger than me, and the two of us loved playing together. (Her living with me also made it to the bad list for other reasons; when a child moves into your home and it becomes more theirs than yours within weeks, that's pretty traumatic!)

2. On my tenth birthday, I got a yellow outfit with a fruit print, and a boy called Jamie who lived up the road said I looked nice when I wore it. I thought I was going to marry him and spend my days in his swimming pool with his perfect family, and that I would live happily ever after.

3. When I stayed with my mum once in the summer when I was about eight, she took me to a car-boot sale in Birmingham and bought me some purple velvet shoes with a tiny heel and a huge diamanté buckle on the front. (This also went on the bad list because when she dropped me home, I was told they were ridiculously inappropriate and they were immediately thrown away. I remember trying – and failing – not to cry when my mum called and asked me if I had worn them lots. I got in trouble that night with the neighbour from over the road, because she said I was a spoiled brat.)

Writing things
down has always
been a great
tool for me.

4. My mum bought me a huge hi-fi in a wooden box when I was about twelve. She bought me Whitney Houston and Tracy Chapman albums on tape, and when I went to bed I would play 'I Will Always Love You' and 'Baby Can I Hold You' on the lowest volume, crying myself to sleep because I missed her so much. Weirdly, this didn't cross over to the bad list. Sometimes, it's good to feel!

5. On Friday nights, my dad would come home and take me, my brother and the neighbour's two children to a swimming pool with a wave machine, and afterwards we would eat burgers and chips and drink Coke in a glass with crushed ice through a straw. My mum and dad's best friends Ron and Peggy would come with their son Aaron, whom I loved, and it reminded me of when we were the happy family that we never were. I would sit in the bar on my dad's lap and hug him, and he would hug me back, and it felt good. They were the best nights in the whole world.

6. On Saturdays, I went to work with my dad alone. We would drive all over Devon, and he would fit new taps and fix toilets. I got to play with his customers' kids and eat cake that old ladies had made. We would always pick up a hitchhiker on the way home, and he would chat to them. We would never drop them off 'on the way'. Instead, he would drive them to where they needed to go, and when we dropped them off, he

would say, 'You learn the most important lessons from strangers' – one of the very few things he got right in life. When I had my dad to myself, away from everyone else, he would tell me the best stories and do the best tricks, and make me laugh till I cried. He played 'Roxanne' by The Police at full blast in his van, and we would sing along to it together, and I felt like he loved me. Like he really loved me.

Writing down these memories helped me then, and it helps me now.

Making changes

And then it was 1997. I'd spent ten years in that home, my family broken or gone, with the neighbour from over the road. I look back now with pride. I hope you do the same, when you look back at the choices you've made, and how you handled the outcomes. During that decade, going from tiny child to teen, I didn't give up, I didn't give in and I played the game . . . At least, until I couldn't any more, and I left the care of the neighbour from over the road, and I left the family home that was never really a family home.

I remember the day I walked out of that house for the final time, and I looked at that mahogany mirror at the bottom of the stairs where my dad had sat that long-ago morning, still hung upon the wall all those years later. I looked at my reflection in the smeared, dusty mirror, and I realised it had looked like that since my mum had left ten years earlier. Sad, unkempt and broken, pretty much like the rest of the house, and exactly how I had felt for years.

Another letter to my younger self, aged fifteen (the day after I left home and moved into my eldest brother's flat)

Hey Girl,

You did it. Well, not quite; we've still got quite a journey ahead of us. But we're over the first hurdle. You need to let go of the hate for her, all the anger. Harbouring all these horrid feelings will stop you from being free, from feeling better, from becoming happier. She was never your stepmum. One day, you will understand the importance of this role, and appreciate what a privilege it is to raise children that didn't biologically come from you. When you understand that, you will see that she was only ever the neighbour from over the road. She never promoted herself above that. She doesn't deserve a space in your brain – especially one where she continues to hurt your heart and your mind.

Forget that now; forget her.

Welcome to your new home. You'll be here for months, not forever. Your big bro is your hero, but right now he's saving himself. He hasn't got the time, the skills or the finances to save you too. You'll have a year of foster care when you leave him soon, going between different homes, different families. It will be OK. Manageable. Better than where you've been. And you're going to love one of your foster carers, Linda. She is the cutest Scottish woman with long, curly hair, the kindest eyes and the biggest smile. She will have to deal with her own problems, which will explode shortly after you move in with her, meaning you have to move out pretty quickly, but one day – when she is in a better place, and so are you – your paths will cross again, and there's going to be a love there like you've never felt before.

This time next year, you're going to be living in a bedsit. It will be clean and warm, but it will also be lonely. because it's the first time you've been alone, properly alone. At night, when you're falling asleep, you'll be left with your thoughts, questions that no one will ever answer, and there will be a sadness some days that you can't shake off.

I want to tell you that plugging yourself with drugs vaginally and carrying them on trains for men in their forties is a bad idea, as is trying to shake bad feelings by snorting class-A drugs or downing alcohol. I want to tell you that these things won't fix anything, that they'll just give you more unanswered questions to deal with, and still no one to answer them. But I know it's pointless, because you won't listen. You're in survival mode, and you need the £50 they'll give you to pay your bills. So instead, I'm just going to let you know that this is all temporary. In about fifteen years, things will be OK. You're going to bring some little people into the world, and they will give you strength you need to keep going, to keep fighting your way out of the trenches.

When you move into your bedsit, you'll feel cut off from the world because you don't have a landline phone. To contact your friends or family, you will have to walk ten minutes to a payphone. That will make things even harder, even lonelier, but this too will be temporary. Soon, mobile phones will be invented – and then something will happen called the internet. Both of these things will have their bad points, but they will also give you a lifeline. They will help to save you and change your life.

For the next few years, you're going to feel like a shitty human a lot of the time, but you're not. You just behave in a shitty way sometimes, because you're a little bit broken and have no idea how to deal with your trauma. Every time you make a mistake, you'll learn something – you're learning as you heal. You're evolving and growing, even when you can't feel it. And one day, quite a few years from now, you will read this letter from me and think, 'Shit. I did it.' I promise you that.

So, right now, I need you to believe that promise, because over the next fifteen years, there will be times when things feel so dark and heavy that it will be nearly impossible to keep your faith in me. You won't see the point of your existence, and the guilt you will carry for the decisions and choices you are forced to make will consume you. Keep this letter safe. Read it. Read it again and again. On the bad days. On the days you're loaded with shame, on the days you're questioning everything that you are and everyone that surrounds you.

Remember this is a journey. In order for you to get to where you need to be, you'll have to fall down so low that you'll feel like you're underground, like you have to dig your way back out, both for yourself and, one day, for your babies. And when the tunnel of darkness seems never-ending, I promise you, I swear to you, there is a light at the end of it that is burning so bright. You've just got to keep heading towards it, even if you have to crawl. Don't give up and don't give in. You deserve that light, and so do your babies.

I love you, and I will write to you again in 2024, just before you turn forty-two. There will be a reason for that – it will be pretty special. Massive hugs. See you in a few decades.

Big Rach (but still not big enough to always know better) xx

You are not a shitty human being

When I think about the decisions I had to make to survive, some of them make me cringe so hard my toes curl. For pretty much the first three decades I was on this planet, I was really struggling. Writing it all down to share my dark places and coping mechanisms with you in this book has also highlighted that I have, so far, spent only a quarter of my life feeling happy and loved. That's hard to face; it's tough to think about the younger Rach who battled through those first thirty years, often alone. And what wrecks my brain the most is that thirty years is a huge amount of time – it's such a significant stretch of my life. Even though 'that life' ended less than a decade ago, I don't recognise the little girl or the woman I was back then. I don't recognise that mother, friend or partner. It feels like I'm looking at someone else. I struggle to feel any connection to her, because deep down, I still spend much of my time feeling ashamed and embarrassed of who she was. But I shouldn't. I can't. And I hope reading this book will help you to overcome negative emotions you've been holding on to about yourself for too long as well. We have to own our pasts in order to move forward to a better future – and often, owning our pasts can be really uncomfortable.

The good side to all this reminiscing is that I can acknowledge that, *finally*, I've pretty much stopped making shit decisions and taking shit actions – most of the time. It still happens occasionally. We all have relapses and make mistakes, don't we? That doesn't make us shitty human beings; it just means we can sometimes do slightly shitty things. So we have to forgive ourselves.

For the last ten years out of my forty-one on earth, I've been surrounded by (mostly) safe people who have my best interests at heart, who scrape me off my bedroom floor when things feel too much, and who genuinely want me to do well and succeed in life. They want for me what I want for myself: self-worth, strength and power.

You have the power in you

To write books like this, which I hope will resonate with readers like you, I have to remember the little tricks and things like the above – letters to myself, timelines, living in denial at moments when it's needed – so I can share them, and teach you how you can help yourself. In the following pages, I will be opening up my box of the survival tools I needed to survive in the hope it will help you not only survive but thrive, just as I have been lucky enough to do over the last ten years.

We have to own our pasts in order to move forward to a better future.

For you to benefit from what I write, for you to identify with my life and use my experiences to help your own make sense, I have no choice but to revisit difficult scenarios and situations. I will remember words once spoken and screamed; I will recall incidents that were terrifying, and choices I made which today knock me for six. And I'm OK with that, because I know the me from back then isn't the me today . . . but she has a lot of lessons to share.

I hope this book allows you to feel helped, heard and motivated, just as I do when I come across honest people who talk or write about things they have done or are doing that people could judge – or even hate – them for. These truth-telling warriors are brave. It's hard to stand up and tell your truth – I know it is! But if sharing my journey can help just one person feel less alone, ashamed or frightened, if it can raise awareness for others, then I am here for it. I used to spend too much time worrying about what people thought about me. I'm getting better at that now. Today, I am more concerned with what *I* think about me. I hope *The Power in You* encourages you to feel the same.

The book will be split into three parts.

- 💜 **Part I: YOU** will be focused on how my mistakes and moments can help you find your own power. I'll share stories and anecdotes from my life, past and present, that will highlight what to do or what not to do when you're trying to regain control and find your voice. It's an assortment of all the tips and tools I've gathered over the decades to grow my confidence and self-awareness.

- ♥ **Part II: FAMILY** will be focused on bringing that same power to your family unit, in whatever shape or form that takes, with stories and advice on children, parents and siblings. I'll tell tales from my family home today, with all the love and drama that entails, talking about my life as a mum and stepmum, and sharing how I've handled various parenting challenges. I'll also think back to my own parents and siblings, and the things they have done that still affect me – positively and negatively.

- ♥ **Part III: RELATIONSHIPS** will focus on relationships with romantic partners and exes. I'll share with you how I found resilience and independence at last, after years of not loving my body, and enduring abusive relationships. I'm a survivor, and I'm here to help any of you who find yourself in a similar situation.

In all three parts of the book, I will take you through my past and my current patchwork life, giving examples of the challenges I've navigated, or am still going through. This book will be about mending hearts, healing pasts and making fresh starts. It will offer real-life examples of how to cope with change, how to manage disappointment, and how to find your team and make it work. As humans, even if we were raised by incredible, loving, supportive parents in a safe, warm home, we still fuck up. We still make decisions that hurt others, sometimes destroy others. We can do things that hurt the people who raised us, and at times even ourselves. But there is always hope, there is always love, and there is always kindness. Most of all, this book will be about finding the light in the dark – and appreciating everything you have. You earned it.

Let this book give you the space to ask questions, dig for answers, educate yourself, apologise (if you feel you should) and change (again, if you feel you should). Let's face it, most people will occasionally remember something they did or said before they fall asleep at night which makes their belly do an anxious flip, or they might have a flash-back on their commute to work to a bad decision they once made that makes them feel like they're going to vomit.

We are human.
We sometimes do and say terrible things.
We learn from our mistakes.
We behave better going forward.
We learn to love ourselves and other people.
We find our power.

Go with it. Read my story, think about your own, and learn to love your life, no matter how it looked 'then' or how it looks right now.

Good luck.

There is always hope, there is always love, and there is always kindness.

PART I: YOU – FINDING LIGHT IN THE DARK

Today, my life is pretty ordinary, although I imagine to many people who are on the outside looking in, it doesn't seem like that. They see the social media posts about book deals and events; they see the brand deals I get, or my clothing line selling out in minutes, and assume that's how my life looks. But it isn't. It's mostly about the family I've created with my Josh and our kids, in our home. It wasn't easy, but I got there. And in the first part of this book, I'm going to share the tools I have used and the lessons I have learned that got me here, including writing, therapy, getting rid of toxic people, and dealing with toxic guilt.

As I meander through my stories here, think about your own life, and consider whether the things that have worked for me or others could also work for you.

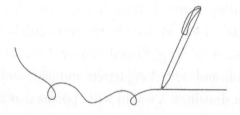

Writing: Hope on the page

Today, my life is at its most ordinary – and happiest – when I am writing, whether that's for myself or for you. Writing has been like therapy for me throughout my life, even at the darkest times. I journal a lot. I often wonder what Josh would think if I passed away and he read the things I write on my iPad or in the Notes app on my phone. I wonder what he would think of the things I type just for me, that I need to get out of my brain in order to clear feelings of overwhelm, desperation, anger and sadness. I wonder if he would question my thoughts and feelings, ask why I look at things the way I do, or believe that I am somehow different in this world where I lose myself in my writing compared to how I am in real life. I imagine some things would make him laugh, some would make him sad, and some would make him wonder why I didn't say out loud what I had on my mind.

Yes, writing is my therapy. It always has been. When my mum left, I would write to her every Sunday with my eldest brother, at his girlfriend's house. I would sit at her dining table and write long letters and lists, and decorate them with drawings. I would write poems that rhymed. I also journaled from a really young age, and loved keeping diaries. I had the famous nineties Filofax, and I had a lockable diary with a little key, where I would write down all my secrets . . . until the neighbour from over the road picked the lock with a Kirby grip and read the multiple pages I'd written about how much I missed my mum, how much I wanted to live with her, interspersed with stick drawings of us strolling together in the street with a bright sun overhead. After that, and the horrific things she told me about my mum, I never journaled again while I lived in that house. I learned that journaling, like so many things, wasn't safe while I lived with her.

When I went into foster care, I began journaling again. I remember the diary I used: it was lilac, with two or three days per page. I needed a page for every day, ideally, but I couldn't be fussy back then, so I made do with what I had. I would try and squeeze in the things I'd done, stuff other people had said, things I'd said, my future plans, hopes and dreams, cramming them all on to a tiny little page. I would use speech bubbles and so many exclamation marks, with love hearts scattered all over the place. I remember when I lost my virginity, I marked the little date box with a green highlighter pen. That was it for the next few years with sex: every time I had it, I would mark my diary with a swipe of a highlighter. No one knew what that meant other than me, until I met my daughters' dad and he found my diaries.

By this point, I had been consistently journaling and writing diaries for almost five years. I loved reading back through them. When I felt sad, or bored, or when I cleaned the bedroom of whatever bedsit, houseshare or flat I was in at that time, I would pull them all out of a big silver Carvela shoebox that sat under my bed, which they shared with hundreds and hundreds of printed photographs, and I'd sit and read them all, grinning stupidly at the good times and feeling sick at the bad times – and often looking at the swipes of highlighter pen, wondering who I'd had sex with on that occasion!

I remember my ex questioning me about the highlighter swipes when he spotted them. I tried to lie at first, saying they marked the dates I was on my period, but it was clear I wasn't telling the truth. Some months I'd have a 'period' every single day, while some days had more than one highlighter mark – and pretty much every single Friday, Saturday or Sunday when I had gone clubbing had a swipe. I had also highlighted the days we'd had sex at the start of our relationship, so he did the maths. This led to one of the most toxic incidents I endured. He made me feel like I'd caused that fight because I'd lied to him, *and* because those little swipes of highlighter pen in five years' worth of diaries showed what a dirty slut I was – I felt so worthless and my diaries ended up in the bin.

I didn't journal again after that for fifteen years. Once again, I learned that although I loved journaling, it wasn't safe while I lived with him.

Today, I journal about whatever the fuck I like, and I write books where I do the same. I'm now at a place, through extensive therapy and hard work, where very little makes my toes curl in shame. I no longer feel like a dirty slut for the highlighter sex swipes – they're a huge part of my story and part of what made me who I am today. I can be the mother I am to my teenagers and parent my kids like I do because of those swipes. I can pump my children with so much self-worth they will never seek attention and love in the ways I did which were often dangerous and left me feeling horrid – instead I am able to approach them with any topic, no matter how big or small and I know they can do the same with me.

Give writing a go – your pen can give you power. Try some prompts here to get you started:

Write three things you are grateful for today:
1.
2.
3.

What does love mean to you and how do you recognise it in your relationships?

_____

_____

_____

What do you most want your family to learn from you?

_____

_____

_____

List three things you would like to tell your partner/children/friends:

1.

2.

3.

Write a letter to someone who has supported you at a challenging time in your life.

Write your own story
I remember in one of my therapy sessions saying I felt totally overwhelmed with work, the kids, the balance of it all: remembering appointments, meetings, double-booking myself, and so on. I was lying in bed most nights listening to Josh sleep thinking things like, *When is Tallulah's*

orthodontist appointment? . . . I need to go to the cashpoint to get bus money out tomorrow . . . I haven't paid that invoice yet . . . Is the family court event on the same day as my publishing meeting? I didn't want to wake Josh by getting out of bed to check my phone and diarise it all, so I would lie awake panicking that by the morning, I'd have forgotten everything that was troubling me (which I always did). The next night, I would lie awake again, thinking of all the same things, and more things besides. It was a vicious cycle. My therapist told me to have a set time each day, but not straight before bed – so, say, between 6pm and 8pm – where I just wrote down everything in my head that was making my brain ache: almost like a 'to-do' list, but one that included thoughts and feelings. The next day, I ticked off what I had managed to do, carried over whatever I hadn't managed to the next list, then added anything else that had come up. It massively helped with the feelings of overwhelm and made my brain feel clearer each night when I got into bed.

This is just one of the many ways in which writing can help us to feel better. Writing down your thoughts and feelings is known to have a healing effect. Whether you make daily entries in a diary or a journal, or keep a to-do list of goals by your bed, writing can help you take stock of what you want or need without input from others, in a totally private space.

Need help getting started with writing? Why not try one of the points below . . .

♥ **Treat yourself** to a notebook that makes you smile and some pretty coloured pens. Keep them next to the kettle for some early-morning goal-setting.

♥ **Write letters to people in your past** whom you have loved and lost, or need to apologise to – or who should apologise to you. Let all the feelings out, then rip up the letter – or burn it, if you're feeling extra dramatic, but risk-assess this first. I don't want anyone getting singed fingers because of the wind direction in their back garden!

♥ **Start a gratitude journal.** List three things you are thankful for each morning, whether it's a new series of *The Traitors* or a beautiful sunset. Read back through your entries when you're feeling doomy or gloomy.

♥ **Imagine you're writing your memoir** – just for you. Go over your highlights, your lowlights and everything in between. This could be a great gift for your kids one day, if you don't mind them seeing you at your rawest.

💜 **If you can't write, draw** – it's another great form of artistic self-expression.

💜 **If you haven't got the confidence to write more, read more.** Find books that will inspire you (ahem!). Find authors who can teach you something, or make you feel less alone.

💜 **Try using a journal with writing prompts.** There are now so many incredible inspirational journals available that help people who struggle to journal. These books ask you questions about your life, past and present. They might ask you to reflect on difficult past events or goals you want to set for the future. They work your brain and help you to explore things you might struggle to bring to the surface without a prompt.

Get to know yourself

Without a doubt, the last eighteen months of my life have been my happiest. I wasn't sure how I felt about turning forty, but it was my favourite 'milestone' birthday yet, and I am in the best place mentally I have ever been. I feel like things suddenly became calmer for me. I accepted that there are some things I can't change; things I'd spent too much time and energy on for too many years. When I turned forty, I let those things go. The relief that came with doing that has been immense. It genuinely feels like two breeze blocks fell off my shoulders and smashed all over the floor in front of me. I want to share some of the things that I've learned or accepted that have helped me get to this place.

Accept your limitations

Don't beat yourself up if you can't do something like everyone else, or you don't finish something when you said you would. We all have limits on our energy, time, money and mental health. Give up seeking perfection. Go for what makes you happiest and healthiest.

Talk kindly to yourself

Too often, we talk to ourselves more cruelly than we would talk to our worst enemies. I remember getting so upset last year because I tried to put on a dress for a night out that I'd worn a year earlier. I'd planned the outfit without much thought. Josh ironed it and, in the lounge, in front of my family, I just started putting it on. I couldn't pull it up over my hips, and it was the first time I recognised my weight-gain in full. I started feeling embarrassed, then I got upset. I felt sick and angry with myself. All these feelings were consuming me – and then the tears came. I started talking to myself out loud. About how disgusting I was, how lazy, how I'd let myself go. And Betsy said, 'Mum, stop. Just stop. You're beautiful and we love you.'

I looked at my three little girls, sitting on the sofa and looking up at me, and I thought, *What the fuck am I teaching them?* They are all told so often by so many people how much they look like me, their mother, and here I am tearing myself (and them) apart. I went and got changed; I sat on my bed and had a little cry to myself, and then I worked on changing my mindset. By September 2023, I had found a gym I loved going to, with a female personal trainer who helped me

♡

Give up seeking
perfection.

embrace my body. My amazing body, that is so lucky to have seen forty-one years on this planet without any concerning health issues. It has delivered four incredible babies and kept them alive with a milk supply. My body is a safe space for so many tiny humans. Yes, it's changing. It's softer, my waist is wider, my tummy feels different, but I'm still beautiful. And now I *feel* beautiful. I no longer stare in the mirror as I blow-dry my hair after a shower, examining the changes to my body which last year seemed so visible and repulsive.

I work on my body so that I can be strong, and I realise the importance of loving myself for me – and for my three little queens, who need and deserve the absolute best role model.

If you're where I was back then, stop it. Talk to yourself in the same way you'd talk to a good friend – with loyalty, kindness and love.

Cut back on clutter

Mentally and physically! If your head and your house are full of too much stuff, you can quickly feel overwhelmed. Be it a pair of old jeans or a negative comment, if you don't love it or need it, get rid of it.

Narrow down nasty influences

Keep negative people and negative news stories to a minimum. Sometimes, it's OK to back away from the horrors of the world and hibernate with cute dog videos on YouTube. Make an impact where you can, but don't martyr yourself and your mental health to every cause and crisis. I've learned that, no matter how much I do, to some people I will never do enough.

It's also OK to not like people. Last week, my friend Laura came to stay. She's a comedian with a huge social media presence. We were talking about everything and nothing, and she said 'I don't expect everyone to like me, because I don't like everyone.' It's the same with music; some of us love old-school R&B and some of us love house music. We all have different interests. It's what makes the world go round. Seb plays rap music constantly, and I feel like my ears are bleeding with it. That doesn't make me a bad person; it just means I don't like it. It's the same with people, whether it's someone you know or someone on the internet. I think we sometimes feel like we have to like everyone, and that if we don't, we're bad people, as if there's something wrong with us. But the reality is, I often see people on the internet whom I don't like. It might be that I don't agree with their content, or it could just be that I get that feeling in my gut telling me it isn't for me. The same is true with people we encounter in real life; there are so many people I don't feel safe around,

Talk to yourself
in the same way
you'd talk to a
good friend —
with loyalty,
kindness and love.

where again that same gut feeling arises. That's OK. It would be a boring world if we all liked the same people. If all artists produced art everyone loved, all singers brought out songs everyone adored, or all content creators created content that resonated with everybody, it would be weird. What would we talk about? How great and perfect everyone is?

The issue, I feel, is what we do when we don't like someone. Perhaps I feel particularly aware of it because of the hate I've felt from others over the last few years. Personally, if there is someone I don't like online, I simply won't follow them on social media. If it's someone I already follow and they begin to irritate or trigger me, I will mute their stories and posts so I don't have to see them. And if it's someone in real life, I will just avoid them. I am at a place now, for the first time ever, where I am surrounded by only safe people, and I haven't 'given myself' to anyone new for many years, because I have been so hurt by people I loved and trusted in the past. I'm not sure I ever will again, if I'm honest – and certainly not while I am working online. What I don't do is hate. I don't seek revenge when someone does me wrong. I don't check up on, obsess over or stalk anyone. I simply remove them from my timeline so their content can't trigger me, or I take a step away from them in the real world.

A lot of these feelings come from me, from where I am, what I have going on, or what I'm going through. It's OK to dip in and out of anything that surrounds you, both on social media and the real world, depending on how you are feeling and where you are in life. That's healthy. What's not healthy is when those feelings consume you to the point of taking over your life – when you find yourself obsessively looking at someone's posts or trying to find out things about someone you don't like. All this will do is have an ever greater negative impact on you. And it can spiral – rapidly.

People can wreck their own lives by being unkind to others. In the past twelve months alone, I've seen so many people get caught for trolling others online. I've seen teachers, nurses, an accountant and someone who worked for our local council lose their jobs because of the things they've said and written about me. I've endured relentless stalking and harassment, with some of these people contacting Children's Services, my kids' schools, and brands and charities I've worked with. There's a line, and they crossed it.

I get that there will be many people who will look at me and won't like me – and that's OK. If that's the case, they should absolutely unfollow or block me. They should mute my posts and stories. And if they know me in real life, I'm fine for them to avoid me or ignore me. This happened recently, when I took Wilby for a swimming lesson and I saw someone I knew, whom I've always spoken to. Our kids are at school together, and they've occasionally slept at each other's houses, so we have each other's contact details. Granted, we haven't spoken in maybe two years, but when I spotted her, I smiled, said hi, then went to give her a hug – and she threw me a look which made me get that instant feeling of panic and sickness, then turned her back on me. Yes, I got a pang of worry and embarrassment. I wondered for a second whether I'd done anything to warrant her behaving like that, but I knew I hadn't. I've always liked her – she's an incredible mum and had always been pleasant to me in the past. But it was immediately clear that, for her own reasons, she no longer likes me – and that's OK. She is entitled to her feelings. So now, when I take Wilby to swimming lessons, we simply avoid each other. I've never heard of her slagging me off locally or online, and she's not outwardly nasty to me, so I just have to accept that I'm no longer liked by her – and I'm at a place now where I'm OK with that. I'm OK with not being everyone's cup of tea, because I know that many people aren't mine. It's just the way the world works.

Find Your Circle

My circle

These days, my circle is much smaller than it used to be, and I'm mostly OK with that. I still have a solid core of incredible ride-or-die friends, but I've learned some really tough lessons over the past few years, when people I thought loved me and had my best intentions at heart went all out to absolutely destroy me. It's especially hard because although it looks like my whole life is played out on the internet, I have never publicly spoken about this. It's hard now for me to know who to trust.

How I survive now is this: outside my own home, I don't tell anyone anything, in person or by text message, nor do I share any photos or videos, without thinking, 'If this reached the public domain, how would it affect me, my kids and husband?' That's not about me not trusting the person I might be sending things to or speaking to, it's about who they're around, who might see or hear it, and what they could do with it. We live in a small town. Everyone knows someone, and it's just horrid when my brain starts spiralling about all the 'what ifs'. Often, no longer being able to forward a text or voice note a rant to someone I trust feels shit. I have a house full of teens, sometimes things get on top of me, sometimes people piss me off, sometimes *I* piss people off – and we all need support from others. We all need to be able to speak to someone who will listen and sympathise and offer solutions. When I'm feeling rubbish, or if I'm questioning something that has happened to me, or I need some reassurance over a disagreement I've had with someone, I need a true friend. A cheerleader. And that's when I feel isolated in this new social media world I have created for me and my family.

I don't really trust many people, not properly, not like I did before. That's not because of anything the people still in my life have done to me; it's not a reflection on them as people. Chances are that if I called any one of those friends and moaned about a row I'd had with Josh, or confided that one of my teens had made a shit decision which had repercussions we were now feeling as a family, or wanted to discuss something that was just not feeling OK to me, they would do nothing but offer me advice and love. They would support me as best as they could, and they would absolutely keep it confidential. This is how my friendships

We all need to
be able to speak
to someone who
will listen and
sympathise and
offer solutions.

have always been; it's what friendships should look like. But my personal experiences have worn me down. Of course, the stuff that has happened has totally changed me as a person. So much stuff I would normally 'blurt out' to anyone now stays firmly inside my head. Often, I find myself about to say something in a conversation, then clamping my mouth shut and mentally reminding myself that not everyone is safe to have these conversations with. That's shit – but it's how it has to be for me to continue to work on the internet. And I think it's a small sacrifice to pay. Every day is a learning day.

I balance this by running an 'open house', an idea that started as a bit of a rebellion to the girls' dad after we left, because he'd isolated me and the girls so much over the ten years I was with him, only allowing me to be friends with people he approved of (and that approval changed like the wind). No one would ever really come to visit me at our home, because they never knew what mood he would be in. When we fled, my best friends Carly and Lianne literally babysat me to ensure I didn't return – and, ultimately, to ensure I stayed alive. They slept over at my flat most nights, especially when Betsy and Lula were with him on his weekends, because I genuinely didn't know how to be alone. I realised how much I love the company of others. Without my best friends back then, I would have 100 per cent have returned to him, as I had hundreds of times before.

And so, our home became 'open'. The girls had friends to stay whenever they wanted; my friends often stayed over, sometimes with their kids. Or I would have their kids so they could work or go out, and I had my nieces and nephews over all the time. It felt good to me, it felt safe and happy. And I suppose it also felt 'busy', which meant I had no time to think about the stuff I desperately needed to heal from.

I continued to have an open house when I met Josh. His life was the opposite of mine. When he lived with his ex and the two boys, they rarely had visitors. Seb had never had any friends to sleep over when I first met him, and people never just 'called in' to their house to say hello. This made me sad. I know Josh trusts less than a handful of people now, and I think he's always prepping himself for the next person to let us down, so he refuses to get close to many people, and when he sees me doing it, I know it worries him, because he's seen the devastation it's caused us and the kids when we've been betrayed by people we not only trusted but loved with our whole hearts. He began training with my personal trainer last week, and when I went in today, I asked how he got on. She said, 'Good, but he's really shy, isn't he?'

Josh is the least shy person I know. He's assertive and confident, so I was surprised to hear him called shy. But when I analyse that, I know Josh will have gone in to train – and only to train. There is no part of him that would have struck up any conversation or encouraged her to ask about him, us, anything. That's because of what we've been through. He is so private; *we* are so private, which is crazy because so many people in this world think they know so much about us. The reality is, they know what we show, and so often these days we don't show the reality, because of the unhealed people who watch us.

Having said all that, I don't want to spend my life alone, without friends, not trusting anyone. I don't want to live in fear of saying the 'wrong' thing, worrying that people might anonymously throw me under the bus. I am a great believer that women need women; there's something about us supporting each other that is so important, and we have superpowers that enable us to overcome the shittiest of situations when we have a good group of women behind us. My issue is that women who were once in my safe group suddenly weren't there for me anymore – and not only were they no longer in my safe group, but they also started to spread gossip about me or my children. It burned, and it has changed me, and my friendships. We've all been there, I'm sure: best friends one day, ghosted the next.

Here are a few of my thoughts on friendship:

💜 I have to remind myself that sometimes people who feel really safe can just stop being that without warning, and that's got nothing to do with me. Something

45

might happen in their lives that just instantly changes them as a person. I know this, because it's happened to me, and if it was to ever happen again, I don't want to be consumed by the fear that they know things about me or the people I am responsible for protecting. So now I think twice about whom I confide in.

- We need different friends for different areas of our lives, at different times. We can forge social connections with people at work, at the school gates, at the gym, at a baby group – they all have their value, and it's a fact that having friends is good for our health. Don't cut yourself off from making new connections, even if you've been burned in the past – just proceed with caution.

- It's not always the other person that's the problem. We need to work on being the friend we'd like to have, too – whether that means checking in, celebrating good news, or offering logistical help. Try to be the friend you'd like to have for those you value.

- If a friendship you love is on the verge of collapse because you need to apologise for something, then apologise. Yes, owning our shit is uncomfortable, but we all have shit to own – and the more we acknowledge that as a society, the less uncomfortable it will become.

- Likewise, accept a humble and honest apology if you feel you still want that person in your life. It's kinder on the heart when you can forgive – but remember your boundaries and your worth.

❤ When a friend shows you who they really are, and it's not good, believe them and run. A bad friend, in my opinion, is worse than no friend.

❤ Don't be fooled by all the smiling girl gangs on social media. Don't allow these inseparable groups of BFFs on Instagram make you feel lesser or unloved. Yes, there are some incredible groups of female friends out there, but there are also some who have enough drama to film an entire *Housewives* series; I know, because I've lived amongst them. Just keep being you and focusing on those you love.

Think about therapy

The person I now trust and confide in the most, other than Josh and the kids, is my therapist Sara, who came along in 2019 and literally saved me. I notice when I've missed just one therapy session, and I believe it's something I will need for the foreseeable future. Spending two hours each week being able to hash out the big and small things with her, talking stuff through, then having hypnosis, is almost like a brain reset. Some weeks, when I felt good and positive, I used to wonder if I should cancel my appointment. I questioned whether I needed to see her. Yet it was often in those weeks I ended up feeling the most broken. I'd go from sitting tucked up in bed, telling Sara over Zoom, 'I haven't really got much to say, and I feel OK,' to being in a total state, the session running over while we worked together to get me into a better place, to get me through the following week until I saw her again. I've told her things I've never told anyone else, and I have never been met with any judgement from her. She helps me make sense of stuff and supports me, allowing me to put problems to bed and teaching me we all have skeletons in our closets. None of us are perfect and we all fuck up as humans.

It's hard work for me to stay as positive as I do. My anxiety is huge when I don't use the toolkit my therapist has given me, and sometimes I can feel it overtaking my mind and body. The difference now, compared to when this first began in 2019, is I know it's temporary. I know my brain is tricking me into thinking I won't cope, and I remind myself I just need to work my arse off to battle it, which I do every single time – because I deserve to be happy, and my kids and husband deserve that too.

A few months ago, I did a podcast with Betsy where we spoke about the effects the trolling first had on me when it started all those years ago. She said, 'You just weren't there at that time. It was like you were there in person, but you were so sad all the time that we lost you for a while.' That was like a knife to my heart, because it was the truth, and I don't ever want my kids to feel I've disappeared again. I don't want to disappear again. Therapy has helped me face up to that.

Josh has had therapy on and off since Wilby was born because of everything the internet trolling caused, but also because we've sometimes found ourselves at loggerheads because we do things so differently. As I shared in the previous chapter, I love an 'open house', and I'd always promised myself that one day, I'd have a house like the one I had for the first four and a half years of my life, when my mum was around, which was open and welcoming to everyone. It's a really different way of living than the way Josh is used to, and I think, over the past few years, the stress we've been through, along with living in this busy home and the worry of everything with Wilby (because we've never done 'neurodiverse' from the age of two together before), was really starting to take its toll on him. Therapy has helped him too.

Don't be afraid to try something new if your old toolkit is no longer helping you. People can sneer at the idea of therapy; some seem to think it's very 'American' and self-indulgent, or a waste of money, because we should all just manage our feelings and learn to cope. But it saved my life. Give it a try if you feel you need to talk to someone different, someone who is trained not to judge, and someone who has taken a professional promise to keep your secrets.

Find peace and quiet

Taking time to be alone: this is a hard one for many of us, especially women. There are so many pulls on us; every hour of every day could be filled doing things for other people if we allowed it. And if we're honest, some of us – me included – don't like being alone with our thoughts.

These days, my home contains all six of our children full-time, two of whom are now adults. But today, as I'm writing, I'm alone in the house. Josh, Betsy and Seb are working, and Isaac, Lula, Edie and Wilby are at school. Sometimes, the emptiness of this house consumes me. Right now, I have my favourite playlist on, full of 'feel-good' songs. I have the washer and dryer going. I like it when the delivery guy knocks on the door rather than leaving the parcels on the step, because it means I get to see another human.

I'm not often good at being on my own, I never have been. Eighty per cent of the time, when I'm not writing books, this house is chaos. It's full of the kids, their mates, their boyfriends and girlfriends. My friends, their kids. Animals. It's busy, it's loud, and everyone needs things from me. I thrive on it, but it also means I'm rarely alone with my thoughts. I don't often get to spend the day with just my brain. And we all need those peaceful, alone moments to restore balance and calm. It's important to carve out some time in your diary to do the things you love, whether that's writing (like me!), walking the dog, taking a long soak in a bubble bath, sleeping, or watching a favourite series or an old film. These are the times we can enjoy being alone without feeling lonely, reflect on what has gone before, manifest what should come next, and daydream about the future.

All the same, my preference will always be for loud, crazy chaos over silence and an empty home. That's my safe place; that's what makes my soul happy. So listen to your soul, and work to achieve the balance of chaos and calm that feeds it.

Know your worth

If, almost two decades ago, when I was lying in an unsafe house, alone and lonely, breastfeeding a tiny Betsy, someone had shown me in a crystal ball what 'today' would look like, I wouldn't have believed them. I would never have believed that what I have right now was possible. I still can't believe it exists. I never take for granted the life we have, but lately, I have begun to recognise and accept that it was me who created it – and I'm also learning it's OK to be proud of that, to be proud of myself.

Josh and I fell in love ten years ago, but he didn't just come along and save me; he was too busy saving himself and his boys. When we got together, we both had to dig ourselves out of financial ruin, and for the first few years of our relationship, we were living hand-to-mouth. We have had to work hard to get to where we are right now. I still have a mortgage, a new kitchen to pay off, and two cars on finance, and nothing about my job is permanently

I know my worth
now. I trust myself
to survive.

secure. If it disappeared tomorrow, things would be tough . . . but tough is OK when you're safe. Tough is OK when you're loved. You can feel things are tough and still be unbelievably happy and content; I know, because that's how it was for the first six years we were together . . . I know I have it in me to keep growing, learning and getting better. I know my worth now. I trust myself to survive.

Find your purpose
(for you and your family)

In my last book, I wrote about Josh starting a career break in June 2022, and how incredible it felt. At the point it started, Wilby was at preschool. This meant Josh could be there for drop-offs and pick-ups, as well as being around for him when he wasn't at preschool. It also meant he was around for the others when they were poorly and during school holidays. It was a huge relief to us, because prior to his career break, when Josh was working as a police officer, he wasn't able to be very flexible, and all the childcare tended to fall to me. This made no sense, as at that time it was my wage we needed most as a family.

His career break continued to feel amazing throughout that year, and also during the summer holidays, when we were able to enjoy our new-found flexibility and do stuff as a family. But it was also tough having Josh around full-time, for all of us. ·

I would love to say things were just rosy, but the reality is, they weren't. Josh had never been around me and the kids full-time. For the first nine years of 'us', he had worked within Devon and Cornwall Police in various full-time roles, and for the first few years we were together, he picked up as much overtime work as possible, anywhere in the country, to boost our income. He was absent a lot of the time, and so for almost a decade, the kids and I had our own routines, our own ways of doing stuff, and it was what we were all used to.

Now, we suddenly had him in our lives 24/7, and it was hard, because Josh likes to be very structured in how he does things, but the rest of us aren't like that. This was easy enough to manage when he was out the house for fifty to seventy hours a week, because we missed him, he missed us, and his 'quirks' (as I call them) were easy for us to deal with as a family because he was only around part-time. God, this sounds awful now I'm writing it down, but I want to be really honest here. I think anyone who goes out to work because they have to rather than because they love it always dreams of a lottery win or receiving a generous inheritance from a wealthy uncle or aunt they know nothing about. They might have this fantasy of no longer having to go out to work, and instead doing whatever they want all day long. When we made the decision for Josh to take his career break, my income meant he could do just that. We felt really fortunate to be in that position, because he'd been working so many hours for so many years to support our family financially, and he couldn't wait to have more time to spend with us all.

When Wilby started primary school in September 2023, it meant he was out of the picture for more than six hours a day. Josh suddenly had all this time – while I was busier than ever. I had just signed this book deal, REBL (my clothing brand) had taken off to the point that I was in shock at the sales, Patchwork House* was as busy as ever, and Jo, my manager, and I had made the decision to get the Instagram home account back up and running, to try and generate some earnings without my face or family being involved, which felt refreshing. We were trying to create a new balance that would work for us. Josh picked up loads of the Patchwork stuff, which was really helpful. He coordinated the meetings, supported the staff with whatever they needed, and helped with the Patchwork Pantry – but it wasn't his passion. I knew he was doing it to help me, and to keep busy, but it wasn't actually making him happy. I kept trying to give him ideas for ways to fill his days, but I had trouble understanding how he was feeling, because I know, if our roles had been reversed, I

---

* Patchwork House is a CIC I opened in 2021. It consists of a women's centre where I employ an IDVA (independent domestic violence advisor) and support staff to help vulnerable women and children like Betsy, Lula and I once were. We run a domestic abuse and trauma course and have a 'free' charity shop and food pantry.

would have happily filled my days with things I loved, or gladly binged Netflix on the sofa and journaled all day.

Josh was *bored*. He was bored of the supermarket shopping, the meal planning and the food prep he did while the kids were at school. Mostly, I think, he was bored of being alone without any structure in his day. He'd been in the army and then joined the police; his whole career had been about routine, timetables and doing certain things at certain times. He was also (as one of his best friends and work colleagues pointed out at this time) used to doing a role within the police that got the organisation incredible results. His passion for the work he was doing before he went on his career break meant the police force were getting some amazing national headlines, and I think going from feeling that buzz to wondering how you're going to fill your days must have been weird for him.

Everything I suggested, he refused. He would say the conditions weren't right for him to go out birding; he stopped going to the gym. By the end of September 2023, things between us weren't great. In fact, they were the worst they've ever been. He was distant and quiet. I was absolutely manic with work, but trying not to be so I could spend more time with him, which in turn made me resent him because I needed to be present within my companies and with my team in order for them to succeed. The more I suggested that he go out, get some exercise, try volunteering somewhere doing something he loved, the more annoyed he became with me. He was also either really quiet around the kids, or nagging them. This meant the kids were coming to me about him because they were feeling the difficulties of change, and if I'm honest, this was a huge trigger to me because of where I've come from.

This continued until, one Thursday afternoon, when the kids were at school, we decided to have a chat about it all. That chat turned into the worst argument we've ever had. We shouted, we screamed, I felt like I was on the verge of a panic attack – and then Josh just burst into tears. He properly cried, huge, fat sobs he couldn't contain or stop, and I realised we needed to change things right there and then, that day, in order for us to be happy and for our marriage to work. And that felt so weird for me – and sad, I suppose, because society always tries to sell us the dream that people who 'make it' don't have to work. It's so common to pray for that lottery win or chunk of inheritance, but here we were, in this fortunate position where we didn't need him to bring in an income, and yet he was the unhappiest he had ever been, and that meant *we* were the unhappiest we'd been since we'd got together. It not only affected us as individuals and as a couple, but also all eight of us as a family.

I thought of all the shit times we'd had together – when he was arrested and suspended under false allegations in 2014, or haemorrhaging thousands of pounds on family court to protect the boys, or when we used to get to the week before pay day each month and realise we had totally run out of money and food. Things back then felt so relentless and hard . . . and yet I remembered how happy we'd been. During those times, we still laughed, still smiled, still found joy in simple things. We were so in love, but more than anything, we were together: fighting, working, overcoming our difficulties.

We all need goals

I remember going on to my Patreon page and talking about our issues, and the comments and stories shared with me by other women made everything feel better. They made me feel less alone, and proved to me once again how women need to support each other and share their stories. One lady told me how her husband had been in a senior management role for a huge corporate company, career-driven and happy; their marriage was incredible and they were financially secure. Then, one day, he was at work and there was an armed burglary. He had a gun put to his head and he thought he was going to die. He tried to return to work afterwards, but she said it was as if her husband had disappeared that day – and he hasn't come back since. He left work for good and has become almost housebound. He is severely depressed, and they are struggling financially, meaning she has to work all hours to bring in an income so they can keep their home.

When I read her story, I knew we had to change things. I knew we had to fight to get things back to where they had always been before we were here. We had to get Josh his purpose back, because that was his power. It was what made Josh *Josh*.

We spoke about Josh returning to the police, but his previous role had been filled, and there was nothing else where he could be behind the scenes that would give him those same highs. We spoke about him volunteering, and he contacted some local places, but they all wanted someone for no longer than two-hour stints, which wasn't what he needed. Then one day he bumped into a friend who told him about someone they knew who wanted to create a new role within their organisation. It was to do with everything he loves in the bird world, and it sounded perfect. A few weeks later (about six months ago now), he began the role. Soon after, he went back to the gym, started going birding in his free time, and the old Josh returned – really quickly.

All of this meant that his days were filled with his own stuff again; he was busy working, so some days, we didn't speak from when he left home in the morning to when he got back in the evening. It meant he'd missed us, and we'd missed him. He felt like he had purpose and structure again. The down side was that we still had teething issues. When it was the school holidays or the little ones were off school sick, we were back to me juggling it all – and that was almost impossible, given my work load – but things felt good again with Josh working; they felt like they used to.

We realised pretty quickly we needed more director-type staff for REBL, and recently Josh made the choice to hand in his notice and come on board full-time there. This means he can ultimately have a job that is based around building our brand, our business. It means that between us, we have the flexibility to manage our children's needs, but now we're both working in an environment we love with an incredible team. I feel like I've got my Josh back: the one I fell in love with. We sometimes sit in a pub on the edge of the sea and watch the waves together, and we talk about everything we're thinking and feeling, and we make plans again – for our future. We each have our individual purpose, but we also share a purpose as a family.

How to find your purpose

Do you have things in your life that help you get out of bed in the morning? Goals, ambitions or even hobbies that fill your heart and your calendar? If not, here are some suggestions to inspire you and help you to regain some purpose.

- **Open up your mind to new things:** Read more, travel more, seek out clubs or groups, in person or online, where you can chat and collaborate with like-minded people.

- **Focus on an area you're interested in:** Research it and find yourself a mentor, someone who can act as a guide and inspiration.

- **Don't get stuck:** Don't fall into the trap of thinking that because you've always done something a certain way, or fulfilled a certain role, you have to stick with it. Change is good.

- **Don't follow the herd:** It doesn't matter if most people don't understand your passion – wood-whittling, anyone? – just do what makes sense to you.

- **Make a list of your childhood dreams:** Write down the things you always wanted to achieve, the things you were good at at school, or the things you've seen other people do that have made you feel tingly with envy or interest. Look at the list and see which of them you could add to your life now.

- **Ignore the cynics:** Sometimes, it's hard for those around you to see you grow, change and improve your life. Your purpose will remind them of their lack of it. Tune them out and keep focusing on what makes you and those you love feel happy and fulfilled.

- **Find your passion:** I'm obsessed with supporting women who are like I once was, and understanding trauma. That's why I opened a women's centre, where I volunteer my time helping others in situations like the one I was once in. Whether you lost a relative to cancer, you're a survivor of domestic abuse or you love animals, find your thing and give it your time. Volunteer, fundraise, raise awareness. I always say there is no better feeling than the one you get from changing the lives of others because you're so passionate about the cause. In helping others, we help ourselves.

Spinning plates (and not panicking when you drop some)

With a positive, there's often a negative – and having six kids with individual needs and personalities can often lead to a very real sense of being under pressure. Life is a balance, and I have to remind myself of that on the days it all feels too much. I am an employer, and I have the luxury of being flexible if I need to be – which is all well and good when I have the *time* to be flexible. In the last few months, I have been so busy. Wilby has had four ear infections, all requiring him to be off school and at home, needing me to be with him as he's been so unwell. There is always something going on at one of their schools; then there's the food shopping, meal prep and other realities that come with running a home that is full of children (and their boyfriends, girlfriends and mates, a lot of the time!). It's hard. It's a full-time job in its own right, but as Josh is also incredibly busy, it often falls to me. I have to bite my tongue a lot, and on some days I angry-cry at how overwhelmingly shit it can feel.

So much of it comes down to what's going on with the kids. When they're happy, so am I, but most days they need to chat something through with me, or need advice or reassurance over something, and it's hard, because six is a big number, you know? You probably feel it even if you're a mum of one or two, or a dog mum. Some days, I feel like I'm one of those supermarket deli counters from the nineties where people used to take a ticket and stand around waiting to be called. I feel like they all pile in from school and it's like, 'BAM. Here we are!', and I need them to take a ticket and just wait for me to finish a session with one, have a breather, then move on to the next.

I never want them to feel I don't have time for them, and I never want to not give them my full attention because I'm simultaneously typing an email, editing a manuscript or sending a voice note. I don't want them to feel I downplay their problems, and I know from what I have seen and heard from other people that the fact they are all still talking to me is a total blessing. All the same, on some days it can just feel like a lot.

I have to remind myself that before I know it, life won't look like it does now. One day, I will get that peace I so often crave – and when I do, I imagine I will be praying to rewind to the days when I felt like the supermarket deli counter! The truth is, we can all get pretty good at spinning plates when we have to – especially if we constantly remind ourselves that it's not forever. I feel like now I've got to the point that I have two adult children (and two more a few years away from reaching their ages!) I know that actually we're going to drop some plates along the way – either them or me, and that's OK. Yes, the plates will smash, make a mess, but to date we've been able to clear them up and to put it right again – even in the times when it felt like we couldn't. We can get over things we think we can't, and situations that feel so overwhelmingly scary and shit do get better. It's time, patience and the realisation that life isn't going to be easy and beautiful every day.

Stop overthinking

You know when you're driving along and you spot a police car in your rear-view mirror, and your heart instantly starts to beat harder and faster? You find yourself wondering if there's anything illegal they'll spot on your car – a brake light out, a tyre with no tread. You start panicking that you might have done something wrong. You start thinking that they're going to pull you over, and your mind races. You begin practising in your head for how you will plead innocence to anything they accuse you of, because you *know* you haven't done anything wrong – and even if there *is* a brake light out, you weren't aware until now, right? Then you see that the police car is indicating; it takes a right turn and disappears from your mirror, and you breathe a weird sigh of relief, smile to yourself and think, 'Why am I such a massive wanker?'

That's how my brain works each and every day, but about life. I constantly feel like this life I have built is all going to go wrong. I wake up from bad dreams about what might happen, out of breath and panicking. It's only been in the last few years that I have started feeling like this; it never happened before. I often think it began origi-nally because of the trolling I experienced. All these anon-ymous accounts making constant threats about showing the 'real me' to the world and getting me cancelled, and it left me feeling so worried and sick. I had always written about my mistakes and bad decisions publicly, I've never hidden them from anyone. There was nothing to reveal. So why was I overthinking everything, and so fearful of being 'found out'?

A huge part of why I began blogging on Facebook all those years ago was because, at that time, all I could see were the happily married mum bloggers, the ones who seemed to have it all together and never spoke about anything like the life I'd had, or that lots of you have had, with the guilt and shame and fights. I remember when I first started researching blogging, and came across the pages of these already successful mummy bloggers, with their positive posts and curated pictures, I felt so alone, so out of my depth, because I had done and experienced and lived through some really horrid shit – and nobody seemed to be writing or talking about that kind of thing. When I first started blogging, I felt sick every time I hit 'post', but before long, people found me online who got me, who'd had experiences similar to the ones I was sharing, and this spurred me on to share more. When the trolls started threatening to 'out' the 'real me', and people from anony-mous accounts claimed to know me and have 'stuff' on me, it was like spotting a police car behind me. Although I knew I hadn't done anything terrible that I was keeping a secret, I still had that underlying worry, that sense of 'What if?'

Nowadays, even though I haven't looked at the content these trolls create for more than four years, I continue to overthink everything, and I wonder if it's a result of those experiences. Or maybe I think everything is going to go wrong because I never thought that all we've been able to achieve over the last few years would ever happen. Perhaps it's because, ever since I left home at the age of fifteen, I have had to penny-pinch to make ends meet, living in survival mode. I was poor for the whole of my adult life, until the year I got my first book deal.

I think those feelings will sit with me forever; those worries of 'This is all going to go wrong' are there because, for the majority of my life, things *have* always gone wrong. Even today, if I notice I have enough money in the bank to treat myself to something nice, I overthink it. My mind says, 'But if you buy that handbag and then you lose everything, you'll regret buying it – you'll wish you'd kept the money in the bank to pay the bills.'

Try to live in the moment

When that happens, Josh reminds me that I shouldn't overthink these things and punish myself. He reminds me of the hundreds of police officers he's worked with that never treated themselves or their families to anything, because they lived for that future day when their retirement would come along and they'd get their lump sum and lifetime pension, at which point they'd plan to travel or buy a little holiday home – but they never made it to retirement, or those who did found themselves in awful health or saw their marriages fall apart, and realised they couldn't fulfil their dreams.

I really try and get in the mindset that life is for living, now, because who knows what's going to happen tomorrow? So many people who create that savings pot to do it all 'one day' may never get that one day. We see it all the time. We hear about it constantly. We all know someone whose life has been tragically cut short, and we think, 'That could have been me.' This should prompt us to change and live in the moment more, but it's hard, isn't it? Especially if life hasn't been easy in the past and you're always trying to plan for the next catastrophe.

I have to constantly remind myself that my life looks like this now, and that's OK. I remember that nothing was ever handed to me (although if it had been, that would be OK too, and probably easier to digest). I've worked hard to get here, I take so much shit every day on the internet to be here, and I deserve to be here. And yes, maybe one day it won't look like this, and things might get tough again financially. Still, some of our happiest times as a family – in fact, probably the majority of them – were when we had absolutely nothing and the future looked bleak. That's because, when life it like that, you find enjoyment in much simpler stuff, like getting a takeaway on a Friday night, or saving up to buy your kid that pair of trainers all their mates have for their birthday.

Remembering this helps me to know we'll be just fine; it helps me to stop overthinking everything and to live in the moment. So if you want the bag, and you have the money in the bank, buy it. And if it all goes to shit, upload it on a selling site, and remember it was nice while it lasted!

Treasure the glimmers

Life is made up of a million tiny little moments, and the happy ones are what can get us through the tough times. I'm working hard on remembering and storing these moments of love and joy, these glimmers, as I create the home I never had for me, Josh and our kids. I want my kids and their friends to remember the memories made there, with us. I want them to feel safe, happy and wanted. These are the glimmers I'll treasure forever. Try to remember yours, too.

Years ago, in our old house, I'd get in from work and we would have up to twenty kids in the back garden, sometimes all the kids from the entire street, jumping on a trampoline or practising gymnastics on Betsy's beam or bars. They'd be making slime with Lula in her shed or creating dens in the trees in the farmer's field at the bottom of our garden. Josh and I were skint back then, but I'd take out a huge jug of squash and a tin of his mum's

Life is made up of a million tiny little moments, and the happy ones are what can get us through the tough times.

famous brownies and enjoy watching them have fun. We left that house almost six years ago, but I look back at the videos of those times, or we bump into one of the kids who used to hang out there with us who's now an adult – some of them have children themselves now – and the memories flood back, for us as a family and, I hope, for them as individuals. I hope we created good memories in their childhoods for them to look back on.

Now our babies are bigger, we create different memories. On a Friday night, we get a takeaway and play board games. They all bring friends or girlfriends or boyfriends along, and the older ones sometimes have a few drinks. Although they're not playing in the garden anymore, drinking squash and eating Grandma's brownies, they're still hanging with us, choosing to bring people they love into our home to create new memories. It feels pretty special that they want that when there's so much else out there available to them.

Find your special moments. Lock them away in your heart, journal about them, and remember them whenever you need a boost to power through a difficult day, week or year.

Ignore the haters

Josh and I went to Poland recently for three nights. Other than going away for two nights for my birthday last May, it's been a while since we've done a trip together where we have time to just be 'us', without the kids. On one of the nights in Poland, Josh pointed out that, bar one pair of trousers, all the clothing I had taken with me was from REBL – my own clothing brand. It really hit me that not only had I created a brand and designed clothing that was successful enough to make up the biggest part of my income in 2023, but I had also created something I loved. I had literally made my own wardrobe. We went back to the hotel and I opened my suitcase and just looked at everything in it other than my underwear and thought, 'That's all mine.' I felt proud, and I realised that with the number of sales we've had, the repeat customers and the feedback, this achievement really was mega!

it's ok to hype
yourself up.

The trolling that has been aimed at me on the internet has definitely made me retreat into my shell over the years. I hate that I've been bullied into not allowing myself to feel proud of what I've achieved because of all that we endure online. But I'm going to say it here, and I want you to feel it about yourself, and your own achievements, big and small. I *am* proud. I'm proud of how hard I work, I'm proud of what that work has created, and I'm proud of my success.

That's OK. It's OK to hype yourself up. It's OK to shout about your achievements. It's a good thing. It's a fucking great thing. And so life goes on, I continue with everything I'm doing right now, and I plan for the future. There's a difference between being a bragger or a show-off, and reflecting on how far you've come and giving yourself a pat on the back. You're making a life that means something to you. Be proud of yourself.

PART II: FAMILY – DREAMS, TEAMS AND RECOVERING FROM TRAUMA

When I'm not working, I spend my weekends with my Josh and the smallest two of our six children, Edie and Wilby, who are ten and four. Occasionally, the others will hang out with us too, but now they're teens and have their own lives, they usually have their own plans – and three of them have jobs – so other than Friday nights, which are 'our nights', it's hit and miss how much we see them. It's strange how you wish the tiny years away, and then miss them so much when they're gone.

I've learned through my own experiences, as a daughter and a sister, and now as a mother and a stepmother, that families either mean everything or nothing. There really isn't anything in between. The family I was born into is fucked beyond repair. They make me feel like the black sheep – and maybe I am. But the family I am making and building and strengthening today gives me the power to heal from the past, and move on to a better future.

Who we are now

I thought an update would be good, a brief overview of where we are right now. It's changed so much since the last book, which seems wild considering it was only a year ago (or two years, by the time you read this!). Many of you are very loyal to us, reading all my books and following @ parttimeworkingmummy on Instagram. Our six children are now aged four, ten, fourteen, fifteen, eighteen and almost twenty. That's a lot of children with a lot of needs, ideas, hopes and dreams. All totally different, yet so similar at the same time. My hardest and most delightful job is raising them.

As I update you on all the kids, you might recognise bits of your own parenting journey in there. I've pulled out some key moments, tools and ideas I've learned from my experiences with each kid, which I hope you'll find useful. At the very least, you might find the stories amusing and get a sense of comfort from knowing you are

There's power in connection and solidarity, especially in the tough and trying moments.

not alone. When it comes to mothering, there's power in connection and solidarity, especially in the tough and trying moments.

Betsy

Betsy, our eldest, moved to Liverpool last winter. She was really struggling mentally, and didn't know what she wanted to do work-wise. She stayed with a family friend and worked between a sports shop and a vegan restaurant in the city. She met some really lush friends and went out loads, and I was really hopeful she would love city life – but she kept going on about travelling. She started saving and, on 23 February 2023, she flew to Thailand alone where she met some friends and travelled for four months, then flew to Australia to stay with some of our best friends who live on the Gold Coast. She was there for another month, and then she came home.

In hindsight, she should have saved for longer and got herself a working visa before she left, because if she hadn't run out of money, I don't think she would have ever moved home. Other than three meltdowns while she was travelling, which happened because she was alone and sick, she was so happy during that time. She spent five months living her best life, then, when she came home to us, she thought things would feel better. She had been gone quite a while, what with her time in Liverpool and the travelling, but the reality on her return was that her friends had just got used to her not being here. They had formed different friendships within her original group, there were new people in her group she didn't know, some of her closest friends were now living with their boyfriends, and they were all either at university or working full-time. When the honeymoon period of being home wore off, which only took a few days, the feeling of 'real life' smashed her straight in the face, and the happy highs gave way to a new low.

She downloaded an app to pick up last-minute shifts working anywhere and everywhere locally, and worked her arse off to get some money in the bank as quickly as possible. She was working all over the place, so was meeting new people and keeping busy, but deep down, she was in the same position she'd been in before she left for Liverpool. She was still just as lost; but now we were almost another year on.

I had to reassure her that things would be OK, that eighteen was such a young age to have your life planned out. I told her I didn't expect that of her, nor did I want it. But she came home to find all her friends at uni or working, settled and happy, and because she didn't feel either of those things, it added to how shit she was feeling. She also felt rubbish because she would see on Snapchat that friends had gone out for dinner or to the cinema, and she hadn't been invited. I think she thought she would come back and just slot back in, but nine months had passed, and for seventeen-to-nineteen-year-olds, that's a mammoth amount of time. It's an age when everything changes.

It was tough for her; some days, it is still tough. She's been home for seven months now and is working full-time as a teaching assistant in a school for children with special educational needs. Right now, that job is the one thing keeping her strong and happy. She gets excited to hang out with her class as she idolises the kids, and her work team are really lovely, but as soon as the weekend hits, she feels low.

Last week, she booked another flight to Thailand. She'll be in Asia for five months, and then she's going to apply for a working visa in Australia. She leaves the UK in October 2024 and she is hoping to build a life out there, away from here. I hope she does. There isn't a single part of me that wants to keep her here close to me, because if there was, it would be purely for selfish reasons – for me. She isn't happy here. She's lost her glow, and Betsy is at her most beautiful when she shines. She shone when she was travelling, she shone when she was around people from all over the world. I truly hope she builds a life that makes her so happy she will shine as brightly as a star.

Lessons I'm learning from parenting nineteen-year-old Betsy

- ♥ Going from being a teen to an adult is really tough, because real life is tough, and I don't think we prepare our kids enough for that. Being an adult is really fucking hard.

Betsy took herself to the GP while I was in a meeting recently as she had tonsillitis, and they gave her a prescription for antibiotics and other medicines. When she went to the pharmacy to collect it, the woman told her the charge was over £20. She called me asking, 'Why are they charging me?' I said, 'Because you're an adult now, babe, and you work full-time.' She was genuinely stunned.

- All of a sudden, they're no longer a kid. It hits them hard that the things that have always been done for them don't get done anymore. The free stuff is no longer free, and they need to start thinking about some kind of life plan, because life is hard and it costs money. That can feel overwhelming. I feel overwhelmed for her, and I'm forty-one.
- Help them understand that real life, as an adult, is nothing like life as a child or teen. It can be such a difficult thing to navigate. Be kind to them – and yourself.
- That saying 'life is a rollercoaster' makes total sense, because it is. You have to teach them that they are not going to wake up and feel happy every day, and that it's absolutely OK to have days where they feel rubbish, overwhelmed or angry at just being adult age.
- Them reaching adulthood can feel like it came out of nowhere to us as their parents, so I can't imagine what an absolute headfuck it must be for them. Imagine spending eighteen years of being spoon-fed a yellow antibiotic by your mum every time you get poorly,

then suddenly having to book your own doctor's appointment, get yourself there, explain your symptoms, get to the pharmacy and then find yourself being billed nearly £20 for the pleasure – all while having the worst tonsillitis. And then you have to remember to take the pills on time, four times a day.

♥ I never spoke about these changes with her, because it's new to me too. I've never had an adult child before. We're both navigating our way through the biggest transition of her life, and I'm realising I need to start having conversations with the others about the stuff I'm learning alongside their big sister to get them ready and prepared. Betsy has been my guinea pig, and I will prepare the others much better. I think they have also learned a lot from seeing her grow.

♥ My job is to reassure Betsy of how proud I am of her. She is working in a job where she's making a real difference to so many incredible little lives, and the fact that she loves it is something that many people don't have in their work. So many of us wake up going to jobs we hate. I've been there many times over the years, and it's the worst feeling. Sunday-night anxiety about returning to work on a Monday after a weekend off is a real feeling.

♥ It's also my job to keep tickling her feet on the sofa at night, and not to get irritated when she asks, 'What do you think I'll do with my life, Mum?' on repeat. My job is to listen.

- ♥ My job is to hold her when the days feel tough and the tears come, and it's also to laugh with her until we cry on the good days. It's about being available.
- ♥ My job is reminding her over and over, like I always have with all of my kids, that everything is temporary. As we've both found out, life goes so quickly – too quickly. This too shall pass.

Before we know it, we will be another ten years down the line, wondering what she's going to do for her thirtieth birthday, and quite possibly having the same conversations about what she's going to do with her life. Or maybe she will be calling me over FaceTime from a flat in Australia, where she's smashing a career she loves and earning incredible money. Maybe she will be living in a huge city, or in a tiny village. Maybe she will be married with a baby. Who knows? I suppose that's the beauty of life: we never quite know how it's going to pan out. We've just got to be patient, hope for the best, and empower our children to forge ahead and make their own mistakes (and be there for them when they do!).

Seb

At the time of writing, Seb is eighteen and in his second year of college, where he's studying media. He has been in a relationship with his girlfriend for about nine months now. She's really lovely and they're good for each other. She stays at our house a lot. They've worked together for years at a local restaurant, so have been friends for a long time.

I get asked so many questions about my kids' boyfriends and girlfriends. People find it so tough to navigate when it happens for the first time – and I get it, because it *is* tough, especially when they break up. I was on my Patreon last week, and someone told me they had treated their son's girlfriend as part of the family for eighteen months, and all loved her, and now they've been left devastated because they found out she's been cheating on him. This lady asked what I would do if this happened to Seb, as she didn't know how to manage her own feelings, or her son's.

Ultimately, Seb's girlfriend is seventeen, and this is the first serious relationship either of them have had. They're not even at the age yet where they have freedom. They can't travel, have nights away or go to pubs and clubs, because she's not legally allowed to yet. The reality is that them getting through the next few years, with the pressures of everything around them, including social media and drunken nights out apart, without making any mistakes is pretty slim. Teenagers do make stupid mistakes, often without any thought or care for anyone else. It's just a part of life. I have seen it, watching Betsy and her friends come in and out of my home for the past few years. I had to help Betsy through her first break-up with her boyfriend of two years, and it was brutal for them (and me!). I have also *been* a seventeen-year-old girl, one who treated my (really lovely) boyfriend at the time like absolute shit, far too often, for far too long.

In an ideal world, Seb and his girlfriend will settle down together one day and support each other through the good and bad times. She loves our family and she's just slotted in with us, which I am aware is a really tough thing for many people to do (I am told we can be quite over-whelming!). But the truth is, they're still babies. They're trying to find themselves right now – who they want to be, where they want to go, and so on – and, just like Betsy, neither of them know what they want to do with their lives. Seb isn't sure if he wants to go uni – and if he does, I'm not sure how it would work. It's impossible to know.

Lessons I'm learning from parenting eighteen-year-old Seb

- 💜 Right now, these two are absolutely besotted with each other, and I hope there isn't a horrid break-up in the future and that they won't hurt each other – but if they do, I'll support them both through that, even if it's her that does the heartbreaking. I've been a teenage girl who's broken a boy's heart, and his mum's treat-ment towards me afterwards made me feel a million times worse than I was already feeling for breaking his heart in the first place. I never want to be that mum. I never want to make a vulnerable teenage girl feel more shit than she already would be.

💜 I never want to hate or judge or turn against someone who's been part of our family for just making mistakes while they grow and evolve, because that is how people learn and become better humans, who go on to make better choices in the future. And if her husband in twenty years treats her like shit, and that husband isn't Seb, I will make myself available to her, because she's one of the very few people that holds a special place in my heart.

💜 I know the importance of having an incredible, fair mother-in-law, because that's what I have in Josh's mum, for the first time in my life. She is there for me always, and she tried to be there for the boys' mum after she and Josh separated. Josh's mum loves very hard and very fairly. I know that if Josh and I were to separate next week, even if I was unfaithful, even if I did some unforgivable shit, she would still do all she could to try and understand. And even if she couldn't understand, she would still see me as the mother of Wilby and someone who has looked after the big boys, and she would always guide, respect and love me.

Right now, I'm unsure of what Seb's future will look like, as is he – but I know it will be OK, because he's a grafter. Just because he doesn't have a life plan figured out, it doesn't mean he won't be successful. Seb has a brilliant work ethic and I know how high he'll fly once he finds his passion. I don't understand how we expect children, at the ages of sixteen, seventeen or eighteen, to make decisions on their entire futures, selecting which course they want to study at college or which degree they want to do at uni. They don't know who they are or what they want yet, because they haven't experienced the world. They don't know what they do and don't like, or who or where they want to be. It blows my mind when people say to me, 'What does your kid want to do with their life?' I don't even know what I want to do with *my* life and I'm in my forties and responsible for six humans.

I'm often in the minority with this stance, as I discovered when Betsy returned from travelling. So many people made comments to both her and me about her 'growing up and picking a career'. She's *nineteen*. At her age, I'd just got involved with a perpetrator and was about to get pregnant with her, then spend over a decade functioning in survival mode. So you know what? I'm OK with the fact that she and Seb don't have their lives mapped out or a career planned. Betsy's job right now, earning minimum wage as a teaching assistant, makes her ridiculously happy. Her mental health and happiness overrule any degree, qualification or salary. For me, the priority is my children being happy. I am not going to force any of them into uni or down a particular career path just because 'society says'. They will find their thing when the time is right – just as I have.

Seb speaks out about not seeing his mum
Seb and I recorded a podcast together recently, and eighty per cent of the questions were about his childhood, his relationship with his mum, and why he lives with us. I didn't know how he would feel about answering them, but I was absolutely blown away by all he said. It's so easy to forget the 'then', because it was a decade ago when it started and seven years ago when it properly ended, but the damage done to him in those few years will affect him for the rest of his life. The stuff that happened during that time will influence his decisions, the way he parents if he has children, and the advice he gives to others, forever. It makes him think about stuff that other eighteen-year-olds, who have been raised in a safe, secure home, wouldn't even question or debate. He is still processing a huge amount of trauma, and he spoke openly about that – which, for a teenage boy, is pretty remarkable.

Obviously, once the podcast went live, my inbox and comments section quickly got hit with the 'What about his mum?' questions and the 'I hope she got help too' remarks. And I get it, because I opened a centre to support women like his mum every single day. In fact, I supported his mum myself for years when she was seeing the boys. But this podcast was about Seb; it was about raising awareness for people who are affected by living with people in addiction. There was so much he said that I watched and listened to over and over – alone, with Josh, with him. I made the decision to cut out his angriest parts. He wasn't happy with that decision, because he wanted them kept in. I understand that – he has every right to be angry, and I didn't want him to think that me removing them was a way of me not allowing him to express what he feels or saying there was something wrong with it. But I explained to him, as I'm explaining here now, that he still has a whole lot of growing to do.

One of the questions on the podcast was, 'Where do you want to be in ten years' time?' Seb's answer was, 'When I'm twenty-eight, I want to be married with a few kids.' If his dream comes true, who knows how he will feel about his mum and this situation then. I know from my own experience that becoming a parent made me look at my parents' decisions in a whole new way. A lot of it made my anger and resentment towards them worsen, because of the immediate love I felt for Betsy. I couldn't fathom how either of them had made the choices they did. But now I've been a parent for a while, I know that I've made some terrible decisions too. I didn't put my two eldest babies first a lot of the time, and I have needed to take responsibility for that. I've craved their forgiveness for things in the past, and owning a lot of that has been really uncomfortable and painful to do at times.

Addiction is one of the most devastating things that can happen, not only to the person going through it, but also to the people who love them. I see it every day. But to the people who have never been addicts, no matter how much research is revealed, they are never going to fully understand it, because they aren't addicts. It's trying to make sense of something that makes absolutely no sense.

Seb is currently in the midst of his biggest physical and emotional transition, growing from a boy to a man. His hormones are all over the place, and right now, his life – as it is for most teenagers – is all about him. He doesn't have the headspace, time, life skills or maturity to make sense of decisions made by others that, once upon a time, broke him really badly – nor should he have to right now. It's hard enough being his age without adding a load of emotional, confusing shit on top of it. But it won't be like this forever, and maybe one day something will happen in his life that makes him question stuff. Perhaps he will want to sit down with his mum and ask her questions. He may make the choice to support her, even if she's still living with addiction – who knows?

Addiction is one of the most devastating things that can happen, not only to the person going through it, but also to the people who love them.

The anger and hurt he feels right now will shrink, which I'm grateful for, because living with those feelings, as I know from my own childhood, only fucks your head up. When I was two years younger than Seb, I used to fall asleep imagining how I would seek revenge on the neighbour from over the road, and on my dad, for not protecting me. I was a broken, angry teenage girl, desperate for something bad to happen to the people who should have loved me. But that hatred I felt inside only destroyed me. They didn't feel it.

I look back now and hate that I wasted so many years, so many hours, so much time, feeling desperate for them to be as unhappy as I was. I hate that they occupied so much of my headspace and consumed my thoughts before I closed my eyes every night. Now, as an adult, being a mum, making my own mistakes, taking bad decisions and having a fuck-ton of therapy have helped me get to the stage where I don't hold any hate or anger towards those people anymore. It was a waste of my time; it ate up so much of my energy. It made me go and score drugs or drink alcohol to numb the shit that was battering my brain, and it made me make more bad decisions because I couldn't think straight. So that's why I don't want to highlight those parts for my kids. I'll validate their feelings, yes, but I don't want them to sit and get comfortable with their rage and hatred. You lose your power if you do that.

I am so proud of Seb, not only for surviving that time but also for, at the age of just seventeen, coming on my podcast and speaking about it all in a way that resonated with so many people living with addiction. I really hope he continues to use his voice, because I know from following people with a similar lived experience to me how powerful it is to see that you can heal from the stuff set to destroy you. A lot of the time, it makes you want to change the world for others.

Lula

Before I begin this section, I want to explain it. I wrote it thinking it would never be published. Whatever I write about my kids in my books always gets signed off by them, and I originally wrote this as a bit of an open letter to Lula. It also felt like a therapy session for me. I wanted her to see my true feelings on things we've been through in the last few years. Not for one second did I think it would end up in this book. She read it in front of me, pausing several times throughout to take a minute, then going at it again.

I repeatedly told her, 'This isn't actually for the book. I just wrote it for us,' but when she'd read it all, we had a little moment together and she asked me to publish it – all of it, with nothing cut out – because she said it was beautiful, that she loved it, and that she hoped that our story might help other mums and daughters. So – here it is.

I met Lianne, one of my best friends, many years ago. We'd entered into difficult relationships at the same time.

It meant we hit the bad times together and could support one another without judgement. We understood each other. Lianne was one of the very few friends to support me constantly when I left the girls' dad. At that time, she had a little boy the same age as Lula, and she would have sleepovers at my flat with him. All the kids would be together and it made me feel safe. It made me stop wanting to return 'home' to him, which is something I sometimes felt like doing when I was alone with the girls. I was so bad at being alone.

Lianne has watched all my babies grow. She's been there from the start. Last month, she spent a few hours alone with Lula, and I received the following text message after she'd dropped her home.

Babe, I can't tell you how lush Lou has become. She's maturing so beautifully – literally had a goosebump moment talking to her with how pure and lovely her mindset and way of thinking is. She really loves you and the pride she has in you is so lush to hear. You should be really proud.

I replied asking her why she'd sent that just before bed as it had made me cry, and she wrote:

Honestly, I told her how proud I am of her and how much I think she's matured. I nearly cried, as I just loved talking to her. She told that when she helped with Wilby once, she realised she should help you more. She stands up for what is right and she's fiercely protective and proud of you. I had such a lovely evening with her.

Those texts just summed up how *I* feel about Lula too. She recently got her autism diagnosis. She is in her first year of GCSEs. In the past year, things with her have started to feel totally different. She is totally different.

I wrote in my last book about the conversation I had with Lula after her pastoral support said she thought she could be autistic. Lula repeatedly said, 'No one sees me,' but couldn't explain what she meant. We both cried so much that day. I felt so much guilt for not seeing it, and she was terrified that if she was autistic, this was her 'forever'; she was afraid that she would never fit in anywhere and it all just felt horrid. I recently watched the Chris Packham documentary on autism, and it featured an autistic girl who didn't get diagnosed until she was an adult. Up to that point, no one had recognised that she was autistic, and she explained how hard it was to live in her brain as a child. After I watched that documentary, I cried on and off for days afterwards. Again, I had this overwhelming feeling of guilt and shame for not seeing something that now felt so glaringly obvious in my own daughter.

Our whole family has known for a long time now that Lula is autistic. Deep down, I think she knew she was autistic, but it's only since her diagnosis that she began not only to accept that she is but also to embrace it. She now says out loud when there is a smell in a room that's making her feel sick, or when the lights are too bright in a lesson. She will be honest about labels feeling horrid in her clothing without the worry people will think she's weird. She will voice when places are too busy or people are too loud and it's glorious to see her knowing that's OK.

Education-wise, she's flying. Not only is this alien to me, but it also brings its own set of challenges. Lula is the first child I've raised who wants to do well academically. She does all the revision, all the homework. She brings her Chromebook in to Josh and me at night, asking us questions about the Great Plague of London and wanting our opinions on religion. She sends me her test results, and I get emails from her teachers telling me how incredibly she's doing. But with this comes the worry of her not getting the results she wants. When Lula revises hard for a test and someone she knows, who hasn't revised, gets a better grade than her, it makes her question herself. She worries about not getting the GCSE results she desperately feels she needs. And this is new to me. I've always had to try and gee-up my kids to learn, encourage them to try harder at school, and explain how mundane and shit it would be to have to do GCSE re-takes. Lula is the first child I've raised who overthinks, worries and panics about not getting the marks she wants. I don't know which is harder, in all seriousness. I worry about Lula's mental health far more than I do Betsy's, Seb's and Isaac's. The thought of her not getting her predicted grades next year makes me feel sick, because I know she's worked so hard and she deserves them.

An example of this happened last week at her school. It was particularly bad as she moved maths groups last year because she didn't like the smell in the classroom. Right now, she hasn't gelled with the teacher she's got (just because of personality, nothing else). The issue is that there is no room for her to move up a set as the class is full. She doesn't want to move back down one because of the smell and if she moves down two sets she can't get above a level five – which, although it is a pass, it isn't high enough for Lula to be happy. When she got into class last week the teacher marked her test paper and it was the lowest mark she'd ever received. This then sent her spiralling because she feels she can't do anything to now improve her grade and she just gets totally overwhelmed.

In science, the lighting is so bright that it makes her zone out and not concentrate. As a result, she misses huge chunks of the lessons – again, causing her to panic about her grades. And so, for the first time that I've seen, the education system as it is to some children – no matter how academic they are, no matter how much they want the grades and their behaviour is incredible throughout all the time they're there – it just isn't suited to them. The environment just doesn't work for so many children and that's not OK, it's unacceptable that we're not in a position to offer education to all types of children, no matter what their needs are.

It's a different experience to have a child desperate to do well in their GCSEs, and for me it feels much harder. As I said, I know my kids have a good work ethic. They like to have nice things and go to interesting places, and they've been raised by two parents who have worked hard to achieve what they have. I don't get stressed out if they don't seem arsed about GCSEs and grades, because I know they'll find their 'thing' in their own time. They are fun, kind people who will be an asset to whatever they choose to do once life makes sense to them. But Lula? She wants it *now*, and I worry about the effect it will have on her if she doesn't get those grades, and how we will navigate that, because it was never something I worried about as a sixteen-year-old, and it's not something I've had to parent before.

Lessons I'm learning from parenting fifteen-year-old Lula

- 💜 What I do know about her, like all the others, is that she will be OK. We will be OK, and we will get through anything together. I tell her over and over again that this is all temporary, and I know it's gone in, because when everything feels too much for her, she will say back, 'It's temporary, Mum,' even mid-meltdown. It's like her mantra, and it keeps her focused and going during the tough times.

♥ Hopefully she will smash her grades out of the park and will continue her little life journey however she wants that to look. If not, we will come together to work it out and guide her. She has the most wonderful support network around her in her siblings to scoop her up when she needs it – they all do. As much as I hate it when that needs to happen, it's also really beautiful to watch them all rally round and pick up the pieces for each other when they need it.

♥ I've learned it's important to make sure we do stuff together, just the two of us. We go to Costa and get toasties and hot chocolate; we go to the Range and Home Bargains and buy scented candles; and every single week, we buy each other a bunch of flowers.

♥ We've learned to talk openly and honestly with each other, and we now understand each other like we never did before. And this has made us both really happy. Fifteen is a tough age. They are grown-up in so many ways, but at the same time they still need you in – even if they try and fight it.

♥ Sometimes something happens that rocks us to our core as parents, makes us retreat into our shells and feel like we've failed badly, but the reality is we haven't. We think we're the only ones who are dealing with this, but the truth is we're not – we just don't share it, because of shame and fear of judgement from others, especially those parents who look like they're getting it just right. This means that the majority of the time, we go at it alone, which makes us feel even worse. So, believe me, most parents of teenagers will have been through the tough times, too – the mood swings, the resentments, the shocking stories. You're not alone. Try not to judge.

Sex (and love) education
Lula is just fifteen.

She's been in a relationship for over eighteen months (with a break-up of a few months in the middle). It's important to mention, because it's over a year out of the fifteen she's spent on this planet, and teenage relationships are one of the toughest, weirdest things to manage, to know how to get right. You constantly feel you're getting it wrong as a parent and, once again, it's something few of us ever discuss. We all pretend it's not happening, so no awareness is raised. We all feel like we're alone and drowning, and so something that so many of our kids are doing is hidden for fear of what others will think.

Lula and her boyfriend had been together for six months when he ended things. Her broken heart was trampled on by what felt like a stampede of bison, and I genuinely didn't know how to fix her. I couldn't get her to get out of bed, I couldn't get her to go to school. She wouldn't eat, she couldn't sleep, and it was one of my lowest times as a mum – and without doubt one of my scariest.

One day, I heard her talking to Betsy on FaceTime. Josh was doing the school run with the others, but Lula was refusing to go to school again, and she was fully losing it in her room. She was crying so much that she was gagging, and I could hear Betsy saying, 'Tell me what's wrong.' Lula was saying, 'I can't, because you'll be disappointed in me.' That was enough for me to know she'd made some decisions that she was really sad about, that she was ashamed of, and I knew she needed me to be a mum that met her without judgement or a screaming match. I went into the room and sat on the bed with her while Betsy stayed on FaceTime, and Lula broke down and told us why she felt as bad as she did.

What she shared that day remains between us but was I gutted that my teenage daughter had made a decision to do something without speaking it through with me first? Yes. Was I concerned that she had done something that felt so huge at such a young age? Yes, absolutely. I'd had 'the chat' with Betsy and Seb when they were this age, and I'd half-expected to hear about these things from them, because they were out with groups of people, getting up to stuff I questioned regularly, and they loved loving and being loved. It was always a worry for me, but weirdly both of them came to me and spoke to me first.

Lula hates affection most of the time. Hugs and kisses are always on her terms, and even when she willingly gives them, they're often awkward and clumsy. She's always been academic, and hated the stuff her mates got up to, to the point she would tell me in front of them how gross they were when they got drunk or vaped. Having a conversation about this wasn't something I thought I needed to do with Lula at this point – not because these conversations can be uncomfortable, but because in my mind, she was the sensible one. She was the one I never would have thought would have done what she'd done. That's what I was gutted about, more from my part than hers – that I hadn't even thought to raise or discuss it. That's what hurt my heart and made me question myself as a mum, question my relationship with my daughter. Not only that, but I was also absolutely heartbroken.

I now understood Lula's heartbreak. I understood why the messages she was getting from girls and boys in group chats were battering her mental health: because they were name-calling her for a situation about which they had no idea. I knew that the support she now needed to survive the shame she may feel (about a decision she had made at such a vulnerable age) was on a whole new level. She needed to have so much love and self-worth pushed back into her by me, her mum, so that she knew I would be here to talk through any big decision or choice without her going through stuff alone.

And that was it, I think. That's when our whole relationship changed. It's when she changed as my daughter, it's when I changed as her mum, and I think that choice she made, which caused us so much heartache and hurt, actually made us. It's made me parent her totally differently, and our relationship is now so honest and open that, at times, Josh covers his ears with his hands, shouts, 'Just stop talking,' and runs out of the kitchen. But that's what I need, it's what she needs, and hopefully it will mean we will never again get to a point where she feels so sad she can't see a way out, and I find myself desperate to fix a situation but out of my depth because I have absolutely no clue what's going on.

It has also prompted me to have some conversations with Isaac. Even though I don't think for a minute that he's making these choices, I am also aware that I thought that about Lu, and she was. It also means conversations will be happening with Edie ahead of time. Like everything else with raising these babies we have, it's a lesson learned for the future.

A few months later, when things felt better, Lula told me she wanted to try again with her ex-boyfriend. Immediately, Josh and I were against it. If I'm totally honest, the thought of seeing him again made me rage because of the things that had happened and the pain it had caused Lula, but then I gave my head a shake and remembered he was at that time a fourteen-year-old lad. If this was Seb a few years ago, or if it was Isaac next year, what would I have needed from his ex-girlfriend's mum? I would need her to put her feelings aside and focus on what was best for her daughter and him. I would need her to understand he wasn't horrid or nasty, he was just a teenage boy trying to navigate his first relationship, along with all the weird thoughts and feelings that come along with it.

In an ideal world, I thought it would have been easier if he'd just left Lula alone, but they made the decision at the ages they were that they wanted to get back together. I could have told her it wasn't allowed, I could have banned her from seeing him. I could have threatened to remove her phone if I caught her contacting him. I'd be lying if I didn't admit that all these things went through my head. They were conversations, disagreements and ultimately arguments Josh and I had about the situation – but the reality was they got the bus to and from school together every day, they were in the same friendship group, and so many of their friends had homes that were often without any parental supervision that they could easily meet up with each other without me even knowing.

I had two choices. Lock her up like Rapunzel, dish out a shitload of threats and strict rules, monitor her every move and hope she complied – or try and continue as we had been, being truthful and honest with one another, and managing the situation in a way that was as grown-up as possible (for both of us!). I decided on the latter. I already knew if I chose the Rapunzel option, I'd lose her – she would lie to me, hide things from me, and we would be in a worse situation than we'd been in when it all began because I wouldn't be able to support and guide what I didn't know. And I couldn't go back there. I wouldn't go back there.

I called his mum, who I didn't know. For this to work, we had to be on the same page, and she had to know what I knew. I had no idea if she'd believe me, what she would do with the information I was giving her, or if it would make things worse for my daughter. Despite feeling sick as I waited for her to pick up the phone, I trusted my gut that I was doing the right thing. Whenever I'm in a situation, I do the 'Put the shoe on the other foot' scenario in my head – often, it makes me change the way I look at things. That day, I knew it wasn't even a choice. This was her son, after all. Luckily, she was kind and understanding, and we agreed the four of us should meet. Fair play to him, he faced me when he knew I was going to be pretty pissed at how he'd treated my daughter. We all spoke, together and individually. I was really honest about how Lula couldn't go through any of this again, and I wasn't up for them being in a toxic relationship and it's not something I was about to support. His mum was super lush and supportive.

And we started again. It was hard at first. The kids weren't keen on the idea of him coming into the house. A lot of stuff had been written about Lu on Snapchat by people at both their schools (I really struggled to get my head round this too), and her siblings felt angry. Him coming for dinner wasn't something that was welcomed by anyone in the house other than Lula, Wilby and me. Her boyfriend knew that, and, fair play to him again, he accepted it and he worked hard, knowing it would take time for it to be like it used to be at our house before he ended their relationship, leaving Lula so hurt. Betsy was particularly brutal; Edie came in a close second. Although I understood why they felt like they did, I didn't like it. It didn't feel good in our house at that time but now – all these months later – it's fine.

When it all came to a head all those months ago, I thought I'd failed Lula, and I felt sick for weeks, praying people wouldn't find out. But fast-forward a year, and everything feels better, better than ever. Right now, she could be spending her weekends getting high, getting drunk and having regular underage sexual encounters with various lads, like so many teenage girls do, like we all did at that age, and like so many do today – but she's not. Something which, when it happened, felt like the worst thing in the world, has actually been the making of her. Of us!

If you're reading this right now and something has happened that has made you feel like the shittiest mum in the world because you didn't see it coming, I need to make a few things very clear:

- ♥ I hear you.
- ♥ It will be OK.
- ♥ Arm yourself with a shitload of patience and understanding.

- 💜 If you feel like you've lost your kid, like you're a million miles apart and you no longer know them, hang on in there! Meet them with love, even when that's hard to do . . .
- 💜 . . . and then love them some more. Even when they meet your love with rage, anger or silence, they still need it. They need to know you love them and that you're there for them, especially when they're feeling at their worst.
- 💜 You are still their safety net. Make them feel safe. One day, probably when you're least expecting it, your child might fall from somewhere high, and they'll need nothing other than the safety net of you to catch them – I promise.

Isaac

I wrote in the last book that we'd been having a tough time with our fourteen-year-old and his behaviour since starting secondary school. The worst was the night we got a call from his school to say there was a serious sanction for him because he'd been caught fighting on CCTV. I remember crying to Josh in our room. I was so worried. We had never seen any behaviour like this from Betsy, Seb or Lula. Josh, as always, was rational and calm. He pointed out that Isaac had joined a school where his brother was in the oldest year, and that perhaps he thought he had to live up to that. Isaac was also in a totally different place to where Seb had been at that age. So much had changed in the few short years since Seb had been his age, with new social media apps being used by everyone and infiltrating their brains. Josh said he was hopeful Isaac would get all his bad decisions out of the way at a young age, then sort himself out by the time he reached Seb's age.

And sure enough, over the last year, Isaac has totally turned things around. Obviously, there's a chance he could return to making choices that are far from ideal, but for over a year now, he's been well-behaved. He has lush friends, has joined a local football team, and sets his alarm for 6am most mornings so he can work out at a gym before getting the bus to school. With our other five children, it's easy to write lots about them, as they have so much stuff going on, but with Isaac, it feels so simple. He is just easy and kind and doesn't give me headaches or make me worry like the others do . . . sometimes that in itself feels like a cause for worry, though! He is almost adult-like in terms of his opinions and his understanding of stuff. Even when he's acted like a bit of a dick, it's possible to have a mature conversation with him about it. I always say to him, 'If this was happening with your son, how would you manage it?' I feel like when I say that to all of them, it makes them see things differently. It certainly works with Isaac. He owns his shit and he learns from his mistakes, and that can make him feel like a breeze to parent. He has lost that teenage know-it-all gobby attitude that Seb still has moments of today, at eighteen.

As with Seb, parenting Isaac means looking at how addiction can impact on people's lives. Let me tell you more about what I mean.

One morning last year, Isaac came down to the kitchen looking upset. He showed us text messages from a number he didn't have stored. They were from his mum. They had been sent in the middle of the night. She had also left him voicemails, calling several times at around 3am. He sat on the sofa in silence at first, looking at the floor, shrugging his shoulders as if to say he didn't know how he felt about it. His hands were clasped together and resting on his knees, but he was bouncing his legs up and down with the adrenaline that was so clearly pumping through his entire body. Then he looked up to the ceiling, and I knew what was coming, probably before he did . . .

Seconds later, he collapsed on to Josh, and I watched his heart break *again*. It reminded me of all those years ago, when we'd told him he wouldn't be seeing his mum again. Trying to swallow away the lump in my throat wasn't going to happen; Josh was biting his lip and trying to hold back his own tears. But I knew that neither of us could – and there was nothing wrong with that. So the three of us cried, feeling it all together, because the situation was sad. More than sad – it was absolutely soul-destroying. Her messages were repetitive and made no sense. Both the texts she had written and the voicemails she had left were chaotic and all over the place. If she was truly well this is not the way she'd have gone about reaching out to her son.

The following morning, I came downstairs before I woke the kids for school. They charge their phones in the kitchen on school nights, and I saw a missed call and a voicemail on Isaac's phone. It was her again. The voicemail was similar to those that had been left the night before, but she also started to say things that were upsetting. I called Josh, and he asked me to delete the message. Nothing good would ever come from Isaac listening to it. When Isaac came downstairs, I explained what had happened. He said he wanted to block her number and not speak to her, as he felt from the messages he'd already heard that she wasn't in a good place. I suggested we could change his number if he wanted, but he said he wanted to see if blocking her would be enough, or if she would try again using someone else's phone or a withheld number. That was the last time we heard from her.

Lessons I'm learning from parenting
fourteen-year-old Isaac

- 💜 Maybe one day, we will be able to help him rebuild a bridge to his mum. If she is in recovery and works hard at getting well, they could reconnect. All I want is the best outcome for everyone involved.

❤ I've learned to try to put myself in the boys' place. I imagine the boys growing up and one day, in years to come, getting a call to tell them that she's passed away – how would that make them feel? Would they carry guilt for not seeing her? Not knowing her? Not reaching out? If they grow into adults, and she's still living with addiction, would they feel better having contact with her to just 'check in', so that when that day comes, they know they had some kind of relationship with her? I'm always trying to think ahead on their behalf, and that's partly because I have the experience of having such a dysfunctional relationship with my own mum, so I'm aware of the feelings that has left me with over time.

❤ I know I don't have all the answers – and that's OK. I don't know what the future holds. I know right now that Seb is too angry, Isaac is too young, and she is still unwell, but one day in the not-too-distant future, they will be grown men, and when that time comes, Josh and I will be there to support them in whatever they decide.

❤ Too often, we don't delve into how we feel or give ourselves options based on how we might feel in the future when certain things happen because it's too uncomfortable or painful – but we should.

❤ So many of us have weird, crazy and odd relationships with our parents, and we all manage relationships with dysfunctional family members differently. There should be no judgement. There is no 'right' or 'wrong' way to do stuff; we do what is best for us, what causes us the least pain, even if we know one day it could end in more pain.

I never feel anything other than sadness for her now, and for them. When they achieve something amazing, when Josh's mum comes over and says, 'Look how they've grown again,' when it's only been ten days since she last said it, or when I just catch sight of them and see how beautiful they are, I feel sad for her that she has missed out on six years of them. This year, Seb passed his driving test and turned eighteen. He is becoming an adult, and I feel gutted for her that she wasn't there for that, because in an ideal world she would have been. I truly hope one day she will be well enough to be a part of their lives and their futures. For now, as I've noted in previous books, I have no idea what the future holds, but whatever the boys choose, whatever they decide, they will have my full backing, love and support, and they will forever be met without any judgement. That is the biggest gift I can give to them as their stepmum.

Edie

Wilby's loyal, devoted and loving big sister/bodyguard is now ten, and still stays at her dad's every Wednesday and every other weekend. I never take for granted how lucky she is, compared to her four big siblings, that she has two parents and step-parents who love and prioritise her needs above anything. Edie and Wilby are the only ones whom I don't study during certain times of the day and wonder how affected they are – and always will be – by their past parental trauma. With the older four, I worry that they lie awake at night and wonder why they weren't enough? Are they sad, angry? Do they want to ask me questions but don't know how to? Do they blame Josh or me for any of it? I have had awful dreams over the years about it all.

When Edie is at her dad's and Wilby asks for her, and I say, 'Dee Dee is at her daddy's,' he laughs hysterically, points to Josh and says, 'You're such a tricker, Mummy.' He has no understanding that Edie has her own biological dad, a whole other family, and I wonder if he will ever get it. Edie, on the other hand, does get it – she gets that her four big siblings don't have the 'other parent' like she does. She cannot fathom why, when her own dad idolises her so much, her two beautiful big sisters, who she adores, have a dad who chooses not to see or speak to them; she's the same with the boys. She questions me so much on all of it. I think she has reached an age where she carries a certain guilt that she has a relationship with the parent she doesn't live with, and her big brothers and sisters don't. It's hard trying to break it down and explain it all to a ten-year-old. I get it, because it's not something I can make sense of, either! Even as an adult, I struggle to understand the way my own parents let me down, and the ways in which the parents of our four incredible older children have let them down. It's something that shouldn't even occupy Edie's brain space, but it does, far too often of late, and I hate that for her. I hate that at such a tiny, young age she carries these emotions about what her siblings are going through. I genuinely thinks she looks up to them all with such adoration that she cannot work out how someone related to them can bear to live without them. It blows her brain. She feels so loved by her dad, and she loves him so much, and she hates that they don't have that.

She'll be starting secondary school in September 2024. How is the little girl that once stood on the kitchen table doing 'pout and peace' when I started my Facebook page all those years ago now about to go to big school? That might be my biggest lesson in this book, guys: time flies! The bad things will be behind you soon, so keep holding on . . . but some of the best times will be behind you, too, so treasure them now. I remember when Josh and I first got together, we would eat at Morrisons Café every Monday as a family treat. The kids loved it because we were 'eating out', and we loved it, as kids ate free with an adult meal. Old ladies would walk past our table and say, 'They won't be this tiny forever,' or 'Make the most of these ages,' or they'd tell us how they wished they could turn back time to when their own children were small.

Back then, I wished I could make the clock turn faster – some days, it didn't feel like it had turned at all. Trying to manage five small children with individual needs, wants, personalities and opinions felt relentless. Everything was hard, keeping on top of the house, going to work, managing tea times, bath times and bedtimes. It was all stuff that we needed to 'do' for them as parents because they were so little – and now they're not.

Lessons I'm learning from parenting ten-year-old Edie

- Ten years have flown by, and I wish I'd listened to all those little old ladies. I wish I'd soaked in a few more cuddles on the sofa and films under blankets. I look back at that time, and just remember always being busy. The windows needed cleaning; the bathroom was grim. I was forever changing bedsheets, dusting, vacuuming. I was too busy too often doing stuff that now, I realise, didn't matter. Put the duster away. None of my kids remember what the house even looked like, let alone how clean it was!

- Edie was born sassy, and we cry with laughter when we play old videos from 2014–2017; she was so little, but she had so much to say. Take the videos. Take the photos. Save them all.

- It's OK to mourn the kind of mother you were when they were little, and to mourn the little kids they once were. I've realised that the hard days back then were actually easier than the hard days we have now, and I mourn those days a lot. I'd give anything to go back and spend a whole day together with them still being those tiny little people. I would watch all the dance shows and plays they rehearsed for hours; I'd embrace bath time and bedtime and dinnertime.

❤ So, if you have small ones right now, and your days all roll into one and you're wishing life would fast-forward, stop. Believe me when I see you running round the park trying to catch your mini tribe, and I stop you and say, 'I wish mine were that small again.' I really do.

Wilby

We've had a rollercoaster with Wilby over the past year. I wrote in my last book about how incredible his preschool was, and we were hoping to send him to a local primary school they'd recommended to us, where a friend's autistic son went. We opted for it, didn't put a second choice down, and then he didn't get in. I was gutted, and my mind raced back to when Betsy was the same age and the same thing happened with her.

She had been at the preschool attached to a primary school I wanted her to go to, and when she didn't get in, I felt like my world had ended. It was labelled the best school in the area at that time, and people would sell their houses and move just to be in the catchment area and send their kids there. I repeatedly appealed. I begged, pleaded and snot-cried to anyone who would listen, but it was a no. I had no option but to look at other primary schools with spaces left. We went to view one and I liked it straight away, so I went out and bought the uniform, ironed her name tag inside, and spent as much time as I could (or as I was 'allowed' at that point by her dad) on weekends and in the holidays hanging out with children who were going there before she started in the September. Then, two days before she was due to start, I got a call to say that a space had become available at the original school I'd wanted. I was in a dilemma. I had spent so long selling her new school to her, hanging out with all her 'new friends' during the six-week holiday, and I had spent a fortune on her uniform, which I now couldn't return as it had 'Betsy-Mae' name tags attached. I decided to stick with the second choice of school. When the same panic started setting in about Wilby, I remembered that fifteen years ago, when this had happened with Betsy and I'd had a total meltdown, it had all worked out for the best.

The difference between my other children and Wilby is that they had a voice. I could ask them how their days had been at school, who they'd played with and what they'd eaten for lunch, and they could answer me. This wasn't possible with Wilby, who was mostly non-verbal. I had a meeting with his SENCO at preschool, and an educational psychologist came in and assessed him. I was really emotional. I went home, sat in my bedroom and cried on my Instagram stories about the whole situation. Locally, lots of people recommended the same school to me. I checked the list I'd been given and it had space, so I went and viewed it. Just like I had when I viewed his preschool, I knew, within minutes, that it was the one for him.

The staff just answered every question I had in my brain without me even having to ask it out loud. It was as if they knew every single worry I had and could reassure me about all of them. Even without his EHCP (Education, Health and Care Plan) he had his diagnosis. They knew he needed extra support, and they promised me, without question, that he would get it – no matter whether they were given funding or not. Their early years head was incredible, as was the deputy head and the teaching assistants.

The school was big, which concerned Josh; there were around ninety children per year and three class groups. Wilby was used to a small preschool setting, and this was going to be a huge change for him. I didn't think for a minute that any choice we made would have felt 100 per cent right, because we hadn't navigated this territory with a four-year-old neurodiverse child before. At times, it brought Josh and me closer together; at other times, it left us at loggerheads. In those moments, I reminded myself that we both had the same end goal: for our son to be happy and safe.

We took him for a 'Parent stay and play' at his proposed school. I could see instantly that Wilby was anxious when other children came into the room. When some of the children began going near the dinosaur toy table that he liked, he tried to block them. Within a short time, there were too many children for him to stop, and Wilby began to dysregulate. Josh bent down to try and distract him, but it was too late. He had gone past the point of being able to stay calm, and he started to attack Josh, punching, grabbing his face and hair, screaming and kicking. His screams were ear-piercing, and I thought I was going to throw up. I had got so much better at coping with him dysregulating in public, but I was already anxious about being there, and whether I would know anyone, and if I did, in what capacity. Because of the trolling we've endured from a few mums at Edie's school, I was super worried about people being unsafe towards us, but I also felt sick about the people who didn't know us, who didn't know Wilby was autistic. I was worried they would label him as the child to keep their kids away from.

I noticed another mum who was there with her little boy. He reminded me of Wilby, and I could feel her brimming with as much anxiety as me. I was aware that if she was feeling anything like I was in that moment, she was probably bordering on tears, so I gave her a smile as we walked out. She gave me one back, and I could see the same sadness in her eyes I imagine she saw in mine. It turned out we had parked near her, and as we drove past her to go home, I put my hand up to wave goodbye and saw she was sobbing. It wasn't a little cry – she was heaving with the same huge, hyperventilating sobs I used to have when I pulled into Costa car park each morning once I'd finished the big kids' school run and Wilby had cried himself to sleep after attacking everyone and himself in the car. Every day, I used to pull into a parking space and just sit and sob, watching him in my rear-view mirror doing his own little sobs as he slept, wondering how the hell I was going to manage all of this forever. It was all just so overwhelming.

Josh pulled over and I got out and walked over to her car. She didn't see me approaching. I tapped on the window then opened her car door. She couldn't catch her breath, and she started trying to tell me why she was crying, but I didn't need her to. I didn't need to hear any of it, because I could feel everything she was feeling. I knew exactly why she was sitting in her car crying while her baby boy was in the back seat chatting away to himself. We had a cry together, I reassured her that I got it, and we laughed about how disgusting our cars had become because of the tiny humans we had created. We swapped numbers. When I spoke to the school the next day, I told the teacher about finding her crying. A few days later, when I went in again, the teacher told me she was going to 'buddy up' Wilby and this woman's son, as they had similar needs and it meant we, as mums, would be together too, with them being in the same class. That made me feel better almost instantly – if nothing else, I knew there was one other mum who would get it. As I've said before, women need other women to be honest with each other and share their stories – even the hardest ones.

Wilby began school that September, and the first week felt brutal. He dysregulated while getting dressed, leaving the house, and on the way there, and by the time he was in the classroom, he needed to use the sensory room immediately. It felt tough, and I couldn't help but question whether the decisions we'd made were all wrong, but his teachers were incredible. I talk at the centre about needing services to scoop up mums who are struggling and make it make sense to them, to give them the support they need so that they can support their babies to the best of their abilities. This is exactly what Wilby's school did. They gave us a later start time and an earlier finish time, and we could do pick-up and drop-off at the main reception rather than the classroom doors, so there were no queues or crowds to make him feel stressed. He continued to access the sensory room whenever he needed to, and the updates they sent were a godsend to us when we were driving ourselves (and each other) insane with all the 'what ifs' about how his day might be going. His teachers sent us videos using an app called Tapestry, so we could see him playing, eating and interacting with new people.

Women need other
women to be honest
with each other
and share their
stories – even the
hardest ones.

And then things just started to get better, and easier, and better still, and easier still. Wilby now goes in and comes out with the rest of his class at normal school times, he hasn't dysregulated to the point of needing the sensory room for a long time, and he is doing things we'd never thought would be possible. They have encouraged him to try hot school dinners. We still send him with a packed lunch every day, but each lunchtime, he chooses a hot dinner, then does a 'sniff, lick and taste' – and he has eaten many foods we never would have dreamed he would even try, including garlic bread, half a meatball, two carrots, pumpkin soup and chicken curry! They fill in a food diary each day that comes home with him, and when he successfully eats and enjoys a food, they take pictures of what it looks like so we can try and replicate it at home. This can be hard, because if he likes a certain food at school, such as the garlic bread, we will need to get exactly the same type at home. If we get garlic bread that smells, tastes or looks different, not only will he refuse to eat it, but chances are it will also put him off the garlic bread at school. It's something we've seen with Lula for years; she has huge sensory issues with food, and Wilby is exactly the same.

Lessons I'm learning from parenting four-year-old Wilby

- 💜 Good education settings are worth their weight in gold. Treasure them.

- ❤ Ask questions. Advocate for your child. Trust your gut if you feel something is different about their needs. Have regular meetings with your child's teachers and caregivers so you are aware of any extra help or referrals needed.
- ❤ Connect with parents who are going through similar things with their neurodiverse children. Find your community. I share how Wilby is getting on at school online, because it gives so many other people hope and ideas. Lots of teachers also message me to say they are changing how they do things because of what I've shared about Wilby's preschool and primary school.

Today, Wilby is thriving. I am so glad we had our first school request refused, because I truly believe the universe works in magical ways and he is just made for the school, teachers, class and friends he has right now! I hope this is the start of a happy, settled and smooth education for him: something he, like every other neurodiverse child, deserves.

Neurodiversity

Understanding neurodiverse children – and how to parent them, educate them in schools, and help them feel accepted in wider society – has become a key motivation in my life. Of course it has, when two out of our six children are living with autism. There are moments to celebrate on this journey we're on, milestones that matter, but there are also challenges worth sharing. In this chapter, I'll be going deeper into how it feels parenting Lula and Wilby.

A Letter to Lula, aged fifteen (my undiagnosed neurodiverse daughter)

Dear Lula,

It's Thursday 7 December 2023. It's 1.25pm, and you're sleeping. I just checked on you. I check on you a lot during times like these. I feel like it drives you mad, but I also feel that secretly, you quite like it too. You should be at school right now, studying animal care. Instead, you're at home, because things aren't great at the moment. It's weird how quickly things change. I feel like I'm wading through the trenches, dragging you along with me against your will. It's a cycle we've been going through together for as long as I can remember: you doing well, things looking great, and then you doing not so well, and things feeling frightening. It's a cycle that never gets easier. Some days, like today, it feels worse than it ever did when you were tiny.

This morning, you were sitting on the end of your bed in tears. I could see you were going into a panic attack, and it was physically painful for me to watch. You begged me not send you to school. I knew that not sending you today would mean that tomorrow, your anxiety would be even worse, but when I force you to go, it feels like I'm betraying you so much, like I'm the worst mum in the world, sending you to a place that I know makes you feel such horrid things. I drove you in this morning, because I knew you wouldn't be able to manage the bus. You cried the whole way there, silent tears rolling off your chin while you looked out of the window, facing away from me. You let me hold your hand – it's not something I would ever usually try and do, because I know it normally grosses you out, but today you let me keep hold of you for the entire drive. Your hand was trembling, shaking with the anxiety of me doing the worst thing possible to you at that time.

We got to school and your old pastoral lead came to

meet us. She just gets you. She took us into a private room and said, 'Tell me what's going on.'

At first, I wondered if you'd sound like you were being too sensitive, but right now, a shift is happening within your friendship group. You're alienated, because the other girls in your group are having huge sleepovers at one particular house, where they do stuff lots of fifteen-year-old neurotypical girls do, the same stuff Betsy did at fifteen, but that's not you. They've stopped inviting you. A few of them tell you about the nasty things they've all said about you – and me. This makes no sense to you. In your brain, you either like somebody or you don't, and if you like someone, you don't say nasty things about them. This makes total sense, really, but teenagers who are growing and learning and changing each day don't behave in ways that make sense. They say things that aren't nice, and they do things that hurt other people – even if that person is one of their very best friends. Right now, that person is you.

Betsy went through the same issues as you are right now, but she didn't look at the world the same way you do. She saw the grey areas. So if she fell out with a friend one week because they'd said horrid things about her, she would be friends with them again the following week, and they'd be sleeping over. And I'd often have to remind her about kindness, because when she was upset and angry, she too would say things that weren't nice or kind about her friends. The difference with you is that it's black or white. It doesn't matter how much I try and explain the grey areas to you, because grey areas don't exist to you. You think I'm the crazy one for seeing grey areas; sometimes, I wonder if I am. Your world seems so simple, so refreshing at times. It doesn't matter how much they apologise, or try and be your friend again. When you're done, you're done.

So, when your pastoral lead asked you today what was wrong and you replied, 'I don't have one person here that likes me,' I genuinely felt like my heart was going to snap. When I reassured you that you did, you cried harder and said, 'I don't, Mum. I don't have one person who is my true friend who really likes me. Name me one.'

And I couldn't. I couldn't name one person in that moment who truly had your back. So once again, we had a little cry together, because at that point, I realised you're not being over-sensitive, you are broken-hearted, and me trying to convince you that you are wrong means I'm not validating your feelings. Right now, your feelings need nothing but validating.

And it's hard, because some of the girls who are being unkind to you right now have been a huge part of our family, our lives, and I know it's not the 'real them'. Two of them have messaged me privately to apologise for the stuff they've said, the way they've behaved. One of them has practically begged me to make you see how sorry she is, because she hates life without you in it. And my heart hurts in equal measure for her, because I know her – she's lush and kind and beautiful – but that's easy for me to say and see, because I'm here with forty-one years life experience, and at times *I* was the teenage girl who was an absolute bitch to everyone. Again, I live in the grey area a lot of the time, and it's hard for you, because me keeping in touch with her, with any of your friends whom you no longer class as friends, makes no sense to you. You see this as me being disloyal, not taking your side. But I refuse to be that mum, that adult, that judges and gets too involved and won't see the bigger picture. Because I hope the bigger picture is that one day, you will come back together; you will be friends again. I hope you will gain the understanding that good humans make shit decisions, and kind people can be unkind. I refuse to write people off, because if everyone had written me off in that way when I was your age, I wouldn't be here today to write this to you.

We came up with a support plan. You have a 'safe space' you can go to when it all gets too much, and I have someone who is lovely and 'gets you' to contact at the school. After our chat, you came home with me, because even though we'd talked it through, even though we'd put the changes in place, you were too shattered to stay. You didn't settle until after 11pm last night, and I heard you pacing around the house just after 5am this morning, because your anxiety was through the roof. I knew me leaving you there today, when you'd had minimal sleep and hadn't eaten or drunk anything, wouldn't have been a good move. Instead, we came home together, ate a bacon sandwich in the kitchen, and then you went back to bed while I continued to write.

I remember when you began primary school. You hated it, the same as you hate secondary now. You just didn't fit in. I wrote in one of my earlier books about you not being invited to parties or playdates, so we moved you to another school where you 'buddied up' with another little girl. You two quickly became inseparable, and did everything together. Neither of you had any other friends – then you hit year six, and she made friends with other children, and you just couldn't cope. You chose a different secondary school to her at first, but you didn't fit in, so we moved you again to where she was. It was at this point that both the pastoral lead from your old school and the SENCO at your new school told us they thought you were autistic, with sensory disorders.

It's been hard, and over the years there have been times when you've needed to have time off because of your anxiety over friendship issues. We've always managed it, but things have got super tricky for you again now. I feel like we've gone back to how things were when you started primary all over again. I want to say it's less scary now because at least we know you're autistic, you've accepted it and, actually, over the last six months, you've begun to embrace it. But the truth is, it's still just as scary, because you still feel like you don't fit in, and now your friends are doing stuff that you don't want to do, so you fit in even less – and the way this makes you feel so mentally unwell terrifies me.

I told you yesterday, and I'll say it again now: we are in survival mode for the next twelve months. I know that seems like forever; I get it. But twelve months out of the rest of your life is a tiny amount of time. We will smash the last year of school together. In twelve months' time, you'll be doing your GCSEs, and then you'll be done.

School will be over – *adios*.

That's it, Lu – you will have done it. Twelve whole years, you'll have managed. Twelve years of feeling like you don't fit in, masking who you are to please others. Four school moves.

I'm sorry I didn't spot it. I'm sorry I didn't realise you were autistic until a teacher who had known you less than six months told me over the phone. Things were so hard to navigate when you were growing up, and I believed your anxiety and quirks were because of the relationship you had with your biological dad. The other day, when you scrolled through my camera roll to the videos of you from years ago, you giggled, looked at me and said, 'How did you not realise I was autistic? Look at me,' and I got this pang of sheer guilt, because looking back now, it was so obvious. If I had you again, I would know in an instant. I'm devastated I didn't spot it, because I know things would have looked so different for you, for us, but all we can focus on is the here and now – and right here and now, we need to focus on the next year and getting over the finish line of the thing that has been your biggest struggle since you started: school.

Thank you for teaching me so much. It's an honour to be your mum, and my world would make no sense without you in it.

Mum xxx

A letter to Wilby, aged four (my diagnosed neurodiverse son)

Dear Wilby,

Today is Saturday, 9 December 2023. Daddy and I came and watched your school play yesterday. You were a camel. I didn't know how you'd cope with us being there. I hoped it would be OK, and it started out quite well . . . but then I saw the change in you. What made me happy, through the worry, was that two of your teachers noticed it too. They were there with you, immediately. Calming you down, distracting you and doing their absolute best to support you so you didn't dysregulate. When you began getting upset, I saw your best friend (also a camel) bum-shuffle across the hall, scoot up next to you and tickle your toes. You both had bare feet, and you smiled at him. He began whispering in your ear, then he showed you your camel tail and whispered to you, 'Stroke this.' You began stroking it, and then you began rubbing the soles of his feet, and my heart hurt and felt happy in equal measure. Then it was your turn to say your line, but when the teacher popped the microphone in front of you, you just couldn't do it. You began getting upset, and your friend just snatched the microphone from you without hesitation and shouted your line: 'THE BABY'S NAME WAS JESUS.' He handed the microphone back to the teacher, and then he carried on whispering to you and playing with your tail.

Since you began big school, he has been a huge support to you, to the point that teachers have implemented things to try and get you to form other friendships so you don't become fully dependent on him – just in case he gets poorly, moves school or plays with other children. It's working. They printed off photos of your classmates and you sit with the teacher and play 'Guess the name'. When you get one right, she brings that child over to the table to introduce themselves, and you talk to them. She said she's noticed that since doing this regularly, you have stopped following the one little boy around as much, and now you are becoming confident enough to go up to whatever area you want to play in on your own, even if there are other children there. You are so brave, because I know how frightening this must feel to you.

Yesterday, though, I watched that little boy, distracting you, calming you, doing everything in his power to make you happy, and I was mesmerised. Mesmerised that such a tiny child could have such an incredible understanding and compassion for others that his only goal yesterday was to get you through that play. I realised then why you stick to him like glue: because he's safe to you. It feels strange to be so grateful to a little boy, no older than five, but I am, because he's made your first few months at big school enjoyable. I wish every child like you could find a friend like him.

You've been on this planet now for four years and four months, and what you've taught people in that short space of time is the stuff of miracles. You have made people kinder and more understanding; you've made them want to educate themselves. I went for a massage last week, and the massage therapist told me that she follows my page. She said, 'I'm so grateful you share the things you do, because I've always been the girl that sees a kid screaming in a park, smacking their mum at the cinema, or rolling around a restaurant floor, and thinks negative things, but now I understand that's not the case. Now I ask if there is anything I can to help, because of the things you've said.' I've had the same thing messaged to me a million times. Imagine that, Wilby! The number of children like you, and mums like me, who have been given more support and received fewer stares because I've shared parts of our journey together.

I remember how different things felt for me when I was writing my last book, how frightened I was of what the future looked like for you, and whether you'd fit into a world which – at times – felt like it would never make room for you. But things are clearer now. I've realised there are more good people in the world than bad, and there's far more understanding than I ever knew existed. I still don't know what 'forever' looks like, and I know things may not always be this good. Some days will feel harder, and we will just have to work through it.

Thank you for coming into our family, for changing our whole world and making it complete.

I love you. Goodness me, I love you!

Your Mummy xxx

Recognising progress

I just re-read the chapter on Wilby from my last book, and remembering the thoughts and feelings I had back then makes me sad. I've learned so much since then.

💜 Back then, I was so focused on what others thought that I missed out on so many things with him. I didn't take him out alone for years. We stayed indoors when we could have been out doing stuff he loved, because I knew the chances of him dysregulating were high and I couldn't cope with the stares and judgement. I hate that I allowed that fear to control me. I've got a handle on it now.

💜 I remember sometimes sharing how I felt, and many people telling me it gets better with time, it gets easier, and I would stop giving as many fucks. I didn't believe them; I often felt like they didn't know what they were talking about – but it turns out they did. Now, two years on, things feel much easier, and even when we're in public and Wilby starts to dysregulate, that panic doesn't freeze me. Yes, I still get a panicked feeling, but I don't hear my own heartbeat pounding in my ears, and I don't feel like I'm going to pass out from the worry of what others around me are thinking and saying.

💜 If people don't get it – if they make comments or roll their eyes – that's on them, not me or Wilby. It's about them not having an understanding of other people within the world, and how sad is that for them?

The hard moments

Betsy, Josh and I took Wilby for Sunday lunch a few weeks ago at a local pub. There were two ladies sitting behind us. One was saying her granddaughter was autistic, and she'd told her daughter and son-in-law that they needed to punish their autistic child in the same way neurotypical kids are punished. She was saying her granddaughter plays up to her diagnosis, and that they needed to just tell her what she'd be having for dinner and sit her on the naughty step when she misbehaved. Every hair on my body stood on end and I felt freezing cold. I felt so much anxiety but also anger, because we shouldn't be punishing any child – neurodiverse or neurotypical. Children don't learn from punishment.

I'd be lying if I said I didn't miss the old me as a mum at times. I can never just 'grab and go' like I could with all the others. It's funny, the things I used to take for granted, because they were just my normal. Every weekend morning when Josh was working, I would get a huge bag of snacks, make sure Edie's iPad was charged, and then drive all over Devon to watch Seb play football. If any of them moaned, I'd pop them in the car with the heating on, give them more snacks, and promise them a McDonald's as a treat on the way home. I could stop at a supermarket and whizz in with them all to grab the ingredients for a roast and packed lunch stuff for the week. It never stressed me out; it was just something I did without question, the way we all lived. Then along came Wilby, and BAM! Everything changed.

Now, whenever we leave the house to go anywhere, we have to plan. Wilby has to know exactly where we are going and in what order, and sometimes if that plan changes, it all goes wrong. It can be something as simple as getting stuck in traffic, coming across a road closure and needing to take a different route, or having to make a quick detour to collect or drop off one of his siblings. If

Wilby has something in his brain, then we need to stick to that – and when we can't, we know the shit will probably hit the fan. We have to ensure he has all the dinosaurs he wants. Occasionally, when I've been in a rush, I've made the mistake of packing the dinosaurs *I think* he will want, because they're the ones he's been playing with, and when I've pulled them out in a restaurant, it has caused him to dysregulate because I've picked the wrong ones. I've learned that trying to save time never actually saves time. We have to climb into his bubble and do things his way in order for it to work, and then we get there. We understand him far more now than we did a few years ago, and we're more accepting of the fact that this is what life looks like.

Helping siblings to understand neurodiversity

Our other kids are fully accepting of the fact that things with Wilby can change at any point. When we're out, it's something we all just try and work with him on, together. That's been hard over the years, especially when Edie was tiny. It's difficult to explain why we always do what Wilby wants, whether that means walking the longer way to the restaurant in the rain so he can see the palm trees, driving the longer way to school because he likes the bump in 'that road', or stopping to look at the cats with the waving arms in the window of the Chinese takeaway. It's hard when you've planned a day out or gone out for lunch, and then you have to leave abruptly with a screaming child when it all goes wrong. Whichever one of us tries to intervene could lose a chunk of hair or end up with blood running down their face from the scratches (honestly, no amount of nail-cutting and filing could stop his fingernails feeling as sharp as cats' claws when he is dysregulated).

There's a lot for parents of neurodiverse children to wrap their heads around: denial, confusion, grief, panic. At the beginning, we didn't prioritise explaining stuff to the other kids, because we were trying to survive navigating our way through something we didn't know how to manage ourselves. Once we'd got our heads around it, once we'd begun to accept it, we could then spend time talking to the kids so they had a better understanding of it all. We stopped planning in front of them; we always decided upon the most basic days out, and never said we would eat out or promise them certain activities like we used to. That way, if it all went wrong and we had to come home, they wouldn't feel let down. We started doing stuff apart. I would stay home with Wilby and Josh would take the big ones out, or Josh would take Wilby out and I'd take the others somewhere different. The older kids needed that. They needed the mum they'd had in me before Wilby came along, because when I was around him in public, I wasn't her anymore. They'd lost their calm, chilled mum who could manage five children anywhere with ease and still have a laugh and be fun. I can't imagine what it must have been like for them to watch me when we were out – I was totally on edge, like a rabbit in headlights, often bordering on tears or a panic attack. I had total tunnel vision, trying to be ahead of Wilby's moods and searching for things that could go wrong. I wasn't present with them, because I was so obsessed over keeping Wilby calm in front of other people. I hate that I wasted so many years parenting him like that, and the knock-on effect it would have had with all my kids.

Finding your neurodiverse community

I remember when I first started out on this journey with Wilby, when I first shared my original Instagram story, where I had no clue what was going on, whether he was autistic, and what things would look like for us if he was.

I got so many messages from so many people, but one really stood out. It was from a lady called Nicola (or Nic), an autism consultant who ran a Instagram page called @ buildingthebasics. She was so lovely, supportive and knowledgeable. I replied to her message straight away, and as we began chatting, I was really drawn to her. She was based about five hours away from me, but she offered me so many tips and bits of advice over the phone. I contacted her most days at first. I sent her so many videos of Wilby when I didn't understand why he was doing certain things, asking her if the things he was doing were normal for an autistic child. I sent her videos of his worst meltdowns in the hope that she would be able to help me from hundreds of miles away. I recorded voice notes where very often I just cried without being able to find my words. They were desperate times, really sad and desperate times, and I didn't understand this new life that felt so consuming and overwhelming.

Whenever I shared parts of our journey, I was met with heavy criticism and trolling, and it made me retreat and worry for a while. During this time I relied heavily upon Nic, probably too heavily at times. She always replied to me, explaining things I had no clue about. For instance, once I sent her a video of Wilby getting 'happy hands' when he was excited. In the video, his whole body shuddered, he stood on his tiptoes and his face contorted into expressions I'd never seen in any of my other children, his whole jaw and mouth stretching to the point where it looked like it was painful. Nic was able to explain the reasoning behind why he did this, as well as the reasoning behind dozens of other heartbreaking moments.

In 2022, I did a book signing in Liverpool, and this cute lady handed me her book to sign. I asked her where her T-shirt was from, as she looked really lush. We started chatting, and her girlfriend said to me, 'Do you know who this is?', pointing to the lady. I said, 'No,' feeling a bit nervous, and she said, 'It's Nic from Building the Basics.'

I was *gone*. Before I could even speak, the tears came, and I just hugged her. Josh saw me crying and walked over, and when I told him who she was, he was gone too. The three of us stood there, hugging, while Josh and I had a good cry in front of a queue full of people. It really hit me just how grateful I was for a woman on the internet whom I'd never even seen. Until that point, I'd had no idea of whether she was young or old. I had no idea what she looked like, because none of that mattered. What mattered was what her heart and mind looked like, what she had given to me, to Wilby, to Josh – to our whole family – with her expertise and kindness. Having her there to hug and thank in real life felt pretty amazing.

I asked her if she would write something for this book, to fill part of this chapter with how our journey looked to her. She sent me this letter, which broke me and made me all at once . . .

Nic, thank you. You saved me at a time things when felt so dark I couldn't find the light. I am forever grateful to you.

Dear Rach,

As I sit here to write you a letter, I am a little overwhelmed by the journey we have been on so far, and I know that this letter will cast a light that will continue to shine like a guide for others. A guide that both informs and inspires hope that there are good people who find each other when they least expect it, and are transformed by the very fact that fate played a part in their lives and their paths were intertwined, perhaps for a short space of time, or perhaps forever. I remember reaching out to you a long time ago after a friend alerted me to your heartbreak in an Instagram story. I watched as you shared how your heart was breaking into a million little pieces following a visit from the health visitor, who had advised that there were concerns about Wilby's development and had raised the query about autism. Your tears flowed and each tear reflected the pain you felt, shards of your shattered soul grieving almost immediately for the child that you loved with a strength that was unsurpassable. My heart broke for you and my soul yearned to reach out as I listened to your stifled sobs, expressing a type of pain that had no real words or definition as it was too raw, too new, too indescribable.

Back then, I had just set up a new business, and the world was scary yet exciting as I ventured forth to offer support and advice to the parents of autistic children and young people. I was hoping to transform lives and make a real difference. Little did I know then that our paths were about to cross, and that we each had something that we could offer genuinely to the other, with no demands or expectations. Those gifts that we shared with each other over voice notes and messages in the months to come were the type of gifts that money could not buy;

they were riches worth far more than that. We shared wisdom, hope, serenity, acceptance, trust and love. Neither one of us really knew where the journey was heading, and I don't think we minded the uncertainty. At that point in our lives, for different reasons, we needed each other, and that was enough.

I messaged you and let you know that if you needed help and support in understanding autism and the reasons why Wilby may be responding to his environment in the ways that he was, I was there for you and would help in any way that I could. Within seconds, you had messaged me back, as though you had been waiting for an answer to your prayers. And it was there, in that very moment, that our journey began. When I look back over that journey, I am consistently amazed by the progress that you and Wilby have made. I watch your stories and reels now, still through blurry, wet eyes, but for very different reasons. Just look at that precious little boy, who has worked so hard to progress, to communicate, to learn how to access the world, displaying the sheer determination that he inherited from his mother. Wilby is flying, and he has yet new heights to explore. It is you and Josh who have created a safe space for him to be himself and to flourish and thrive. You stopped at nothing to ensure that he was able to progress, and you never faltered through the hard times, when it felt as though you could not go on. It was love that kept you going.

Looking back, I remember the tearful voice notes that you would send after a hard day and when Wilby presented with challenges that you did not yet understand. He had difficulties moving from one thing to the next, and I explained how autism can often mean that a child or young person finds change too overwhelming as they have a need for sameness and routine. That sameness helps them to find calm, as it is predictable in an otherwise chaotic world. We chatted about how Wilby would become overwhelmed and overstimulated by his environment, and how he was struggling to understand a world that could, at times, appear unrecognisable to him because he was so dysregulated. It was all about enabling him to feel safe and regulated so that he could begin to understand more of the world around him and interact positively with it. It was a slow journey at first, but you and Josh worked tirelessly to provide a stable and consistent routine and to help him stay regulated when transitioning. We spoke about giving Wilby some heavy work activities or giving him a backpack to carry that would help him feel more grounded and, therefore, safer. It was inspiring to watch as you filled a new backpack with his dinosaurs, and off you went. I remember that Instagram story vividly: father and son, hand in hand, walking to the pub for a Sunday roast, with Wilby skipping along with his backpack on, completely regulated and transitioning brilliantly. What a 'wow' moment for young Wilby.

The diagnosis was another poignant moment, as you were so deflated after being told that your baby was autistic, and you seemed so unreachable and so deeply sad. You sent me the reports to look at, and I felt privileged that you shared them with me, that I could share in this part of the journey and help to explain some of the jargon and professional vocabulary that emotionally charges these reports and leaves parents with a certain sense of disassociation. You were thankful to me, but I felt equally thankful to you. That you felt able to trust me and seek support meant so much to me; little did you know how much you were helping and supporting me back then. With each conversation we had, I felt a little more secure in the decisions I had made as I watched you and Wilby grow together and understand each other more deeply. To know I had been even a small part of that brought me such joy. You shared my details many times on Instagram, and each time, I was able to reach out to more and more parents and offer support, living my dream of making that real and awe-inspiring difference in the lives of so many.

A memory that makes me laugh each time I think of it was when you shared on your Instagram stories how Wilby was scratching his body incessantly and often drawing blood, as he was scratching that hard. I messaged you and suggested investing in body brushes for him, explaining that you could use these to try to give him the feedback that he was so desperately craving and hopefully replace the need he felt to scratch his skin. I told you I had seen body brushes in Primark for a few pounds. You later appeared on Instagram thanking me as the body brushes had worked to reduce Wilby's scratching – and you said you had found a lovely ESPA body brush. I laughed out loud, as no expense was spared on our Wilby. Only the best body brush would do.

There have been many voice notes and messages that have passed between us, Rach, and I will be eternally grateful that our paths crossed. You always tell me how much I have helped and supported you and Wilby, and you will always be more than welcome. My life has been enriched through sharing in your journey, and you have helped me too. You made me feel that I was making a difference, and the beauty was that there were times when you didn't even know you were doing it. I will never forget the first time you mentioned me on your Instagram, and my heart leapt and broke at the same time as my inbox flooded with messages from desperate parents seeking solace. Some of those parents I still keep in touch with now, sharing in their journeys also, which has been an honour and a blessing.

I will be forever thankful to you, and will always be there for you and Wilby. I look forward to watching his journey and taking pleasure in his 'wow' moments. Those tearful voice notes have been wonderfully replaced by glimmers on your grid where you now share the progress that Wilby has made, and that makes my heart soar; truly, it does.

All my love,

Nicola x (Building the Basics)

I still get messages from mums who were where I was a few years ago, the ones living in total fear of leaving the house with their children, the ones who have that desperate 'WHAT THE FUCK?' question clawing inside their throat every single day, because they are looking at how their day has been and thinking it's going be like this forever. It's hard to see past that, no matter how many times people tell you it gets better, gets easier. But it does. And parents need to hear that. All. The. Time.

We also need to share the fears and worries too, of course. For example, I'd be lying if I said I wasn't terrified for Wilby as he gets older. I see how affected Lula is by the things that she's trying to get through. School is hard enough even when you fit in, let alone when you don't – and that's why I'm so passionate about raising awareness for kids like Wilby and Lula, so that people see it, and educate their own kids, friends and family about it. Hopefully, by the time Wilby gets to secondary school, the kids and adults he encounters will be far more inclusive of children like him, and he won't feel like Lula has had to for so much of her school life. There should be a place for every single child to fit in, no matter what their needs are. School should be a safe place for our children. They shouldn't feel mentally unwell at the thought of just walking through the door.

We need to prioritise change, and that's on all of us – those of us with neurodiverse kids, and those who witness our struggle.

Recognising the signs

I often look back at Wilby and Lula's journey from the start and hate that I missed the signs for so long – especially with Lula. I know if I birthed Lula or Wilby again now, I would recognise they were autistic far earlier, and I would be the one to notice it. As I've said, Lula's pastoral teacher was the one who recognised it with her, while for Wilby, it was his childminder – and both of those conversations hit me like a ton of bricks. I suppose one of the reasons I share our journey and write about it so much is because I hope it will help other people. I wish I'd had someone to follow online with children like mine. If I'd known more about it, the signs would have been easier to spot, and it wouldn't have felt so overwhelmingly shit when it did come to light.

Realistically, we could have recognised that Wilby was autistic when he was about 12 months old, while with

Lula we could have known from the age of about three, maybe earlier in hindsight. A lot of those early times with her are blacked out in my memory because of the life we were living back then. In all honesty, I parented Lula in survival mode from the minute I took the pregnancy test until I met Josh. Before Josh and I were together, I spent the majority of the time just planning how we were going to get from one day to the next. I wasn't studying her to work out if she was autistic. We were all living under such a huge level of control from her dad that I put all of her behaviours down to that.

Every single day, someone hits my inbox with the question: 'What were the signs you noticed with Wilby?' I still have the list in my Notes app. I started it when he'd just turned two, writing down all the things about him that seemed different to my other children when they were his age. I'm going to share it here in the hope it can be of help to you.

- Smells everything he holds.
- When upset, he falls to floor, hurts himself, and may bite/attack me, Josh or his siblings.
- Hates certain textures (dog's fur, certain foods) – they make him gag/vomit.
- Screams at high pitch for ages and ages.
- Constantly makes high-pitched noises (when he is happy or sad).

💜 Flaps his hands when he likes something on the TV.

💜 Walks fast and non-stop.

💜 Doesn't like it when people look at him.

💜 Has meltdowns in certain public places.

💜 Has meltdowns going into anyone's house (won't stop until we leave).

💜 Hates holding hands (will bite, sit on the floor or attack us if we try and hold his hand in public).

💜 Non-verbal.

💜 Likes repetitive games (stacking blocks, posting Peppa Pig coins, emptying Mr Potato Head, then refilling, then emptying again).

💜 Likes routine (we just went to Liverpool, and while we were there he was so unsettled and didn't sleep).

💜 No danger awareness at all (would walk in front of a moving car).

💜 Becomes transfixed with certain routes/things (trees, signs).

💜 Has tunnel vision (can't be interrupted when he's focused).

💜 Has no idea of what you're saying (for example, 'Get your shoes on', 'Lunchtime').

💜 Runs in circles with his head down on the same spot until he's dizzy and falls over.

Reading that list back makes me feel lots of emotions, both sad and happy. Sad for who I was back when I wrote it, for the dark place I was in, never seeing a way out, and happy, because it reminds me of how far he's come, how far we've all come, how much I've learned and grown as a mum – and how utterly beautiful he is. The holding hands thing used to be really painful, especially when mixed with his lack of danger awareness. He wouldn't hold my hand anywhere when we were out, and would just run into a road or towards a pond. If we would try to hold his hand, he would bite us with all his strength, and scream and cry with anger. The meltdowns would be endless and full-on, and could last all day. It all felt so tiring. I just remember feeling so exhausted.

Now, we can't go out without him holding our hands. If we let go, he fully panics. He needs to be holding hands with both me and Josh, and if his siblings are with us, they have to stay close by. He hates it if they run ahead or dawdle behind. No matter what he's doing, he wants all of us together. The repetitive toy games have remained but changed, if that makes sense. Since I wrote that list, he became obsessed with animals, then went on to dinosaurs, and now he's transitioning to everything Godzilla and Goo Jit Zu. He still likes to line up things in an order he's made in his head, and he becomes transfixed by this. It's intriguing to watch; his brain and the way he plays can be utterly fascinating. He no longer hates the dogs, and he encourages them to sit on the sofa with him. The feel of their fur and the smell of them used to make him physically gag, and he would sometimes vomit when they got too close to him. To cope with them like he does now is just incredible. He is still a total stickler for routine. He needs to know what we're doing when, and he needs to be warned before we do stuff. I could never go into him and say 'It's bath time now,' or 'It's bedtime now.' Instead, we always have to prewarn him by saying, 'Wilby, it will be bath time as soon as this programme ends,' or, 'Mummy is going to finish her cup of tea, then it's bedtime.'

It's strange to look back to when Lula was little and see similar things that we didn't recognise, and the guilt is never-ending when I think back to that time. Lula will melt down over similar things that panic her. For instance, this morning she couldn't find her top brace retainer. Years ago, when she was young, I wouldn't have understood why she was so stressed about it, and I'd have probably thought she was just being a bit dramatic, that maybe she was overtired. Now I understand it, I understand why that's a big deal in her head, so this morning I stripped her bed, lifted up her mattress, put on my torch and found the retainer on one of the wooden slats underneath. Her relief was visible instantly. For her, life made sense again, it had all gone back to normal, it was safe – but years ago, I wouldn't have searched like that when she needed me to. I would have refused, and I would have looked later, when I had time. That makes me sad, because I know now that she must have spent so much of her time back then bubbling with anxiety because I didn't understand her needs. I hate to think of it.

And so it all comes back to how important it feels to share our story, so that other people see the stuff I never did, so that they are able to recognise similar things in their own child far sooner than I did. I hope this will stop other parents from feeling like rabbits in headlights, lying awake each night in sheer terror over what their baby's future looks like.

It's not all bad . . .

Betsy and I often say we wish we had Lula's brain and boundaries, because when something's happened, when someone we loved and trusted has massively let us down, when we've found out people we classed as family have been anonymously trolling us online, Betsy and I go over and over it, we grieve, we go through so many emotions together. Lula doesn't. That's it for her; those people are just no longer safe, and if they were, they'd have never behaved in that way towards us. For her that's it – done. How refreshing that thought is: to learn someone's unsafe, unkind or not trustworthy, and so flick a switch that says 'See ya,' and let that be that.

Wilby's siblings have stepped up to be the best brothers and sisters possible. They learn about and understand his needs, and every one of them knows how to help him to self-regulate when he goes into crisis. I love that for him – and for them. I love that my kids have also chosen partners who get it and love him too, and I hope this continues in the future. I think it will, because Wilby is adored by everyone in our home. He brings us together, and when he rocked into our world almost five years ago, he was definitely the icing we didn't even realise our cake was missing and desperately needed.

Toddlers: Wisdom on the early years

Parenting is forever changing, because kids are always at different phases. Famously, one of the most challenging times on this family journey is when you have toddlers around, so I want to share what I learned was important – and not so important – during my experiences as a toddler mum. The key thing I remember from those days, which can be isolating and exhausting, is that you need to find your people – or person. Someone to bounce ideas off, moan to, share stuff with; someone you can persuade to join you as you head to a park, duck pond or indoor play centre on a grim February morning.

I wrote in my last book about toddler groups. With Betsy and Lula, I went to the same toddler group, on a Friday morning at the local church. The first time I went, I was really young, only twenty-two years old. It was at the same time my sister and her friends were having babies

♡

Parenting is forever
changing, because
kids are always at
different phases.

(they were all around thirty, give or take a few years either side). I remember one of my sister's best friends, Jane. I liked her straight away. She had a beautiful detached house, a new BMW and lush clothes, and her appearance was immaculate, always. But what I remember most was that she had a totally different energy to the other women there. I was drawn to her. She was fun, and I sensed she was similar to me – totally fucking broken, but just better at hiding it. I felt like she was trying to fit in with a group of women where she didn't really belong.

Her husband loved a night out back then, and at that time so did Betsy's dad. This meant when we turned up to toddler group on a Friday morning, Jane and I were both usually pissed off at them because they'd got in in the early hours, or sometimes hadn't come home at all. I could tell that, despite it looking to the world like she had this 'together' family unit, the reality was that things were pretty dire.

During those toddler years, my girls' dad had a gambling addiction. Around the same time, he declared himself bankrupt, which meant the only debit card he could use was mine. I would see the transactions coming out of our account at all hours through the night: £10, £15, £5 . . . It was relentless. When I would leave for toddler group on a Friday morning, he would still be unconscious in bed, usually sleeping off the previous nights' mistakes, and I would check his pockets for cash. One week he had over £600 in his pocket, so I took £200 and went to the toddler group. I told Jane I was going into town after the group to treat myself, and I confided that I always pocket-rifled when he'd been out drinking, keeping small stashes of money for the bad times when he would gamble away everything.

Before long, Jane began to do the same on a Friday morning, and we would strap our babies into their prams after toddler group and walk into town together. The kids would fall asleep and we would walk round the shops and treat ourselves to coffee and a cake, or a new jumper. To the outside world, Jane was this beautiful, happily married mum in her thirties, who had parked her career to stay at home and raise her babies while her incredible husband went out to earn the family a wage. Meanwhile, I was a young mum in her twenties in an abusive relationship – by this point, even though I was just three years in, anyone that knew me, him or 'us' knew that he treated me appallingly and that the relationship was fucked beyond repair.

What helped me to handle those difficult toddler years – and my relationship – was having an ally. Jane taught me the most valuable lesson without saying a word to me: it doesn't matter how wealthy someone looks, it doesn't matter how much they have in terms of 'stuff'; you never know how anyone's life really is.

Fast-forward twenty years from that toddler group, and Jane is still one of my best friends. She's also deputy manager at our women's centre. Turns out, behind the beautiful life she appeared to be living, she was full of trauma from so much stuff she had endured, including being adopted as a baby, finding out years later that her biological parents had died in an

Happiness [is] about finding the thing that puts fire in your belly. It's doing something worthwhile that you know you're good at.

incident together, and then losing her adoptive mum to suicide. She left her marriage, which she meant she lost the huge home and the expensive cars, but what she gained was time: time to grieve, to heal, to make some more bad decisions, but then to go on and find herself. And having done that, she now supports some of the most vulnerable, broken women in our community. When I see her supporting them to make the changes they do, it absolutely blows me away. Happiness isn't wealth or riches, it's about finding the thing that puts fire in your belly. It's doing something worthwhile that you know you're good at.

I look back at those toddler-group years now and realise just how much they taught me. Just being around other mums, seeing how tired they looked, watching them trying to get a bottle in a baby's mouth while the little one screamed for no apparent reason, showed me I wasn't alone. We shared stories about how our kids were sleeping and eating; we discussed the best nurseries or childminders. More than anything else, I felt we knew what the next milestone was, because each week there was someone there who was already going through it. Nothing just 'came out of nowhere', because we were watching these other babies develop in front of us, as they went from newborns to preschoolers.

So, find that tribe. Find that one friend who understands you like Jane got me, who you can trust, and find a wider community who can tell you where to get the best high chair or how to cope with sleepless nights. They'll make the toddler years much more enjoyable – and survivable.

Teenagers: Wisdom
on the later years

We should have a toddler group for teens and young adults, only without the teens and young adults coming along too! A place where all mums and caregivers can come together to talk about the stuff they're going through. Everyone would be honest, and no one would judge. It would be the same format as a toddler group: a few hours each week, with a load of chairs, decent cups of tea, and jam on toast or biscuits, but instead of talking about weaning, the best brand of nappies or whether controlled crying is actually cruel, we would talk about different stuff – like safe sex, consent, drugs, alcohol, mood swings, school, college, uni, work, friendships, relationships. As a mum raising children from the start of secondary school through to where Betsy is now (almost twenty years old), I'm navigating my way through the unknown. Not only do I have minimal people to go to for support and advice, but a lot of what we're dealing with are not the kind of things I can just go chat openly about on my Instagram stories. The teen years are perhaps the hardest, right?

Between all my kids, I've had the following issues to deal with: underage sex, unprotected sex, drugs, alcohol, arguments between friends, breakdowns of relationships. They are an absolute minefield to get through. I have handled this by being open with the kids, and assuring them that they can speak to me, and each other, about anything. I only realise how unusual this is when other people are in the house and I see their faces, or one of Betsy's friends giggles and says, 'I can't believe you say this stuff to your family.' Despite me getting stressed at times when I know what they're getting up to, who they're with and where they're going, I'd still choose knowing over not knowing every single time. I can support them through what I know, I can advise on what I know and I can be there if they need me – if I know.

These conversations can be so important. Say, for instance, Isaac was going to try smoking weed. If the only people he could speak to about that were his mates and the people supplying the drugs, the likelihood is that all of them would be encouraging, and maybe even pressurise him into doing it. He would only see the positives of smoking weed: how cool he would look, how brilliant it would feel, how well he would fit in. But if he knows he can come and chat to me, we can discuss it properly. I can show him on the internet what happens when smoking weed goes wrong; we can talk about the reality of addiction. We can chat about the people we know within our family who have become addicted to smoking weed, and how their lives look. If that's not enough to put him off, then I want to know when he does it so I can be around if it goes wrong – and chances are, the first time you smoke a joint or seal your lips around a bong, it's going to go wrong.

I don't ever want to be the parent who doesn't know, who believes that my kids just won't do it. My kids – and most teens – will experiment with everything. Realism is my superpower. I want to be present. I want to have the difficult conversations. I want to point out the shit bits that no one else will tell them. I want to be a part of all of it.

I'd love to hear from other mums of teens and young adults, because at times I feel so alone. When I needed advice at toddler group because Betsy had bitten someone at nursery, mums would pipe up with a similar story, and I remember feeling so reassured. I heard the words, 'It isn't just me,' in my head every time I spoke out loud. Having older kids feels overwhelming, because I have no Friday morning group to rock up to and say, 'All my kids are vaping, are yours? How can I get them to stop?'

Understanding your teenager

When I think back to being a thirteen-year-old teenager, remembering the stuff I was doing, the things my friends and people in my year were getting up to, I realise that at no point did I think about how my actions would make other people feel – whether it would cause them upset, distress or any other feeling or emotion they wouldn't have wanted or needed. And that's important to remember, because so often when my kids have done shit stuff, I realise I have taken it personally, I've felt hurt that they've done those things 'to me', but none of it was ever done 'to me'. Other than them gauging how much trouble they'd be in if I caught them, I wasn't even in their thought processes, because the only thing most teens think of is themselves. Teens don't have the headspace to even look outside that box. Of course, once they've made that decision and it's gone wrong and they see the hurt in us, they might think, 'Shit, I didn't really think about that,' but the reality is they're probably feeling more pissed off that they got caught – and the next time they're contemplating making another bad decision, they'll just plan better so they don't get caught again. I don't think for a minute that, when the peer pressure sets in, they'd think, 'Last time I got caught, this really hurt and worried my mum, so this time I'm not going to smoke that spliff.' Instead, they're more likely to think, 'Right, I need to stay at a mate's in case I throw up, so she definitely won't find out this time.'

It's taken me a while to wrap my head around that: that none of this is personal; that my kids are still my kids, they're just my kids as teens and young adults. I have to constantly revisit my own teenage years, to remember that I was thinking of no one but myself, and neither were any of my friends, no matter what their homes or families looked like.

So, during hard teen moments, I've made a promise to myself that I won't lose my shit anymore. It doesn't help any of us, and it leaves me feeling so awful. I also remind myself that this isn't about Josh, or me. In fact, it has nothing to do with us. When my kids have made bad choices, the majority of their friends had made the same bad choices alongside them, so this isn't about the way they've been raised, it's not the effects of trauma or anything else I was trying to pin the blame on. This is about kids just being kids.

It's also about social media infiltrating everything they do. It means they are being exposed to so much stuff far earlier than we ever were. Josh always says that he and I were part of the last generation to have childhoods without social media. After 'us', children grew up being around mobile phones, then they got them, and now they have access to tablets, iPads and phones from when they're tiny. When I actually sit and think about that – when I properly think about it – it feels so strange. I imagine how different my life would look if, ever since being a baby or toddler, I'd had access to the online world, everything that's available on YouTube, and then, as a teenager, I'd been able to see millions and millions of videos at the touch of a button across loads of different apps. I imagine what it would be like if my friends were showing me stuff they'd found too. And what if my whole teenage life was online? People taking pictures and posting them on Snapchat, having sly digs at me for re-sharing a wanky TikTok video. I think of what it would be like to be that age, and for everyone to have access to me 24/7 – and for me to have access to everyone else. It's unhealthy. It's sad. It's devastating.

Our teens deserve our sympathy. I look back at so much of the stuff we did as we were growing up all those years ago, before the internet was a thing – for instance, losing my virginity. Other than seeing a few adult magazines on the top shelf of a newsagent's, and giggling about what might be inside them, but not really knowing, we had no idea what sex was. And that meant we had to actually learn how to have sex. We had to fumble about, find out where things were, what felt nice, and work out what we actually liked. Right now, our teens have access to millions and millions of free porn videos. I can't imagine being a virgin, watching those videos and thinking, 'Is that how I have to act?'

It's why I parent the way I do; it's why I'm so open with my kids. They know their mum made mistakes, they know she messed up – but they also know she went on to achieve really incredible things and be successful. I share things with them, at the right times, when they need to hear them, and I make sure we can have open conversations so that I can support and advise them on stuff.

The adults raising today's teenagers need to swallow their awkwardness and be present and willing to have difficult conversations. Meeting your teen with anger or rage if they fuck up will teach them nothing except that anger and rage are acceptable. Yes, when I'm disappointed or upset with them, I absolutely let them know, but I no longer take their bad choices personally. Any child, no matter what their upbringing was like, can fuck up; and child can make one decision that has catastrophic consequences for them and for others.

Here is what I try to remember to do:

- Have regular chats, debates and question-and-answer sessions together.
- Be open and non-judgemental.
- Love them hard – more so on their bad days, when they're harder to love.
- Know that you are absolutely key in raising decent humans who go on to help other humans and be part of the change in future generations.

♥ Everything changes, but it's still fun and beautiful, chaotic and crazy. I'm not the same mum anymore, because I can't parent my children who are now a decade older the same way I did when they were tiny. I have to adapt and go with it. The biggest change is the ways in which they need me. They no longer need me to feed them, dress them or bathe them. They no longer need me to blow-dry their hair or brush their teeth properly. Now they need me to tell them how to handle an argument with a friend, and whether they should go into work with a hangover. They need me to help them find the best car insurance quote or give an honest opinion on an outfit. They need me to mend their hearts when they hurt or give them paracetamol and hot water bottles when they have their periods.

I often remind myself, especially on the bad days, of the changes my kids are going through from the minute they start secondary school. At the tender age of just eleven, they are surrounded each day by kids up to the age of sixteen. This is such a huge change from primary school, and the change I have seen in the four of my six children in the first year they started secondary has been over-whelming at times. It's also during these years that they start the transition from childhood to adulthood, although Lula was having regular periods for her last year of primary school, and all of my girls' bodies started to develop and change while they were in primary.

When we see our kids every day, it's easy to miss even huge changes. Sometimes, when I'm really struggling, or when they're really struggling, I just go back a year in my camera roll, and I watch the videos of them. The changes they go through in just twelve months are crazy. Everything is different – their voices, the shapes of their faces, their bodies – and it reminds me that if all these physical changes have happened, then the internal changes – to their brains, their thoughts, their opinions and beliefs – must feel so overwhelming for them. They change every single day during these years, and at times it just feels so consuming. Absolutely fucking brutal. I talk about it all the time with my kids. I sit and show them the videos on my camera roll from a year before, two years before, so that they can see it too, and acknowledge how they've changed. It's important to remind yourself of this regularly.

Fighting with your teens

I cannot tell you how much I hate it when I argue with my kids – like, really argue. My goal is to raise my children so they like me, love me, and still want to be around me when they become adults and have this choice. The thought of my kids wanting to leave home to get away from me destroys me. That's why I raise them the way I do, making sure that they have space and room to be honest with me, and that they know I am here for them, not just while they're growing but once they're grown. I hope they always look at me as their home, their safe place, even if they go on to have their own families. It's impossible to be a perfect parent, it's impossible not to fuck up and make mistakes, but that doesn't mean you ever stop trying. You have to own your fuck-ups and mistakes, recognise your own behaviour, apologise to and respect your children.

Some of our arguments have made me feel helpless, but I make myself remember that the unrest is temporary, even when my brain is trying to convince me it's not. I have to remind myself that no matter how much I struggle to make sense of stuff and support them, we will get through it. I try to remember another occasion when something felt overwhelmingly shit and we made it through – and usually that 'something' isn't even an issue any more.

Living in a large family

I think it's only when other people point out the enormity of having six children that I remember it's actually a pretty big deal. Last month, Josh and I travelled to London to meet my publishing team to chat through this book. We left at 7am and travelled back that evening, and Linda who was my foster carer when I was a teenager was at home. Josh had made bolognaise the day before, so Linda just needed to cook the pasta and garlic bread, then feed them. I say 'just', because to us it is 'just', but the next day when she came over, she told me, 'I don't know how you do it every day.'

When I asked what she meant, she pointed out she'd had my six to feed, and then Seb's girlfriend and Lula's boyfriend came over, which made eight, as well as herself. She described them all sitting down to eat, talking over each other, the chaos of eight children while she was dishing up, cleaning up, refereeing the banter (which was bordering on a row), then coping with Wilby getting upset when everyone left the table, wailing, 'My family. Come back. Where have my family gone?'

And I realised – that's our life. Our life is usually six to ten children in our home, every single day. Eating, sleeping, showering. Chatting, shouting, arguing, debating – but always laughing. Our life with all these kids is tough some days, but this chaos is all Josh and I have known for our entire relationship.

I spoke to my therapist about what Linda said, recognising the enormity of having six children full-time, plus all the friends, boyfriends and girlfriends they bring along for the ride, and it's made me be much kinder to myself. I've started to acknowledge that it is hard. I have five children with mobile phones who contact me relentlessly, and I have an autistic four-year-old who can be difficult to parent. Every day, they all return from school and college just after 3pm, the same time Betsy finishes work. Some days, it's good, but most days, at least one of them – if not a few of them – will have had a shit day. That might mean they want to tell me all about it, or worse, it might mean that they just come in full of anger or sadness – and then I feel it too. It's like they need me to feel what they're feeling . . .

Be kind to yourself

Parenting is hard. It's hard to be the 'one' for them all, constant and steady, but it also feels wrong to admit it's hard, to acknowledge it's hard. I always felt in the past that I didn't have the right to complain, that there was some rule stating we can't admit out loud how fucking hard and relentless and impossible it sometimes feels. But it does. Having six humans who need me to be there for them every single day is really fucking tough sometimes, it just is, and I wish it was OK for me to complain about that every now and then without feeling guilty – guilty because there are women out there who can't conceive, there are parents who have children with more significant needs than mine, or any other reason that stops me from being honest when I'm drowning. We all should be allowed to say parenting is hard.

Life isn't a competition. Everyone has their own shit going on, and although most of the time I feel so fortunate and lucky and head-over-heels in love with all my babies, some days, I want a break. Some days, I wish I could say how brutally hard being a mum is without being shut down and reminded of how lucky I am. I know I am lucky. I still know that on the bad days. I never don't feel fortunate – but that doesn't mean it isn't tough at times.

We all should be allowed to say parenting is hard.

How to handle an empty nest

My babies are grown, or growing rapidly. I have two adults, two teens, one pre-teen and a baby who's not really a baby (we just have to keep one as a forever baby). So often, you don't even realise when something will be the 'last time'. Think back to stuff you used to do with your child that you no longer do. When was the last time you sat them on your hip while you prepared dinner one-handed because they cried for you every time you put them down? When was the last time you bathed them before they began showering independently? When was the last bottle of milk they had, the last nappy you changed? When was the last time they woke in the night, and the only way you could get them to go back to sleep was to lay their whole tiny body on top of yours, and then just breathe them in? We never see those lasts, do we? You just, one day, spot a mum in a supermarket rubbing noses with her little girl sitting in the trolley in front of her, and realise you can't remember the last time your own daughter sat in the trolley, because she's walked round the store for years, or maybe now she doesn't even get out of the car when you go shopping because FaceTiming her mates is way more fun. I wish I remembered the lasts; I wish I'd known in the moment that all these 'times' were going to be the last, so I could have soaked them up, felt more grateful, realised how much these babies of mine were growing in front of my eyes – but you don't. It just doesn't happen like that.

As well as all the 'last times' we get with our babies, we also get firsts. Some incredible, some unexpected and some devastating. I think one of the firsts that I didn't see coming – and, again, one that no one had warned me about – is when one of my babies left home.

When we discussed Betsy moving up to Liverpool, she wasn't sure, so we decided she would go up for the weekend with her friend to stay with my friend Jenna, who had offered her a room in her house to rent. She went up for Halloween weekend and went to a club, and just loved it. She was buzzing. She came home and was telling me all about how busy the city was, how different the nightlife was, how much she loved the Scouse accent and the way they did stuff at such a fast, crazy pace, which was so different to the way we live in sleepy Devon. She then announced she was going to move up there the following week. And that was that.

Jenna arrived seven days later with her car, we all went out for a last supper, and Betsy left the following morning. I had to go to work at the centre while she was still sleeping, so I kissed her forehead and left, hoping she'd still be at home when I returned or would pop into the centre to say goodbye. She sent me a video of her and Jenna's cars full of her belongings while I was delivering the Domestic Abuse course at the Centre, and I missed her calls as my phone was on silent during the training. I called her back an hour later, but she'd already left and was on the M5.

I left work that afternoon and went home as usual. I went out to the cabin in the garden where Betsy's room had been for the last five years, and realised she really wasn't there any more. I opened her bedroom door, and the emotions hit me like a ton of bricks. Other than her bedroom furniture, everything had gone. She had left, and now there was a shell. Her smell had left with her, and the once cosy, warm and welcoming room felt bigger, cold and echoey. But most of all, it felt empty.

And *I* felt empty. I sat on the end of her mattress and I cried. I sobbed with my whole heart while looking for something to bury my face into that would remind me of her, but every drawer I opened was empty, her cupboards and wardrobes bare. I felt so gutted, so overwhelmingly lonely – even though inside my home, it was still bustling and full of the usual chaos. There were five other children there, along with some of their mates, my husband and our pets. Nothing and everything had changed in an instant. I'd thought knew what was coming, but I'd had no idea these feelings and thoughts even existed. I felt insane for feeling them, because, as so often happens when your babies grow, people stop talking about the things that wreck your heart and brain. I'd had no warning it would hit this hard. I didn't go into her room again while she was away. It felt like I'd self-destruct being in there, because the emptiness of it all was just too much to deal with.

Past traumas can resurface in moments of fresh trauma

I tried to busy myself so I didn't have the time to think, but my brain kept flipping back to when I was growing up without my mum. I would see her around every three to six months, and everything other than her smell would change. I would say goodbye at the end of the summer holidays, and she would drive off with a golden tan and a strappy top, and then I'd see her again at Christmas, and she would be pale-skinned with a thick winter jumper on. She would have grown more lines under her eyes, and her hands would feel softer each time I touched them. I wrote to her every single week from the ages of four to fourteen, and often, when my brother and I pushed the envelope through the hole in the red post box at our local shop, I wondered what she would look like when she picked my letter up from her doormat, hundreds and hundreds of miles away. Was her hair now blond or dark? Permed or straight? Would she be wearing a top I'd never seen before, or one I'd snuggled into in the past?

It was only when I started FaceTiming Betsy each day when we lived apart that I realised how very disconnected my mum and I had been from one another. I cannot imagine what it was like for her to only see me a few times a year from when I was at preschool through to the age of twenty-four. I can't begin to imagine how she ever held it together going three or six months without seeing me when I was four, five, six, nine, eleven, thirteen, eighteen, twenty-one. I went from a little girl to a woman during the years she was absent. It's absurd to think the only things that kept us together were our weekly letters and a phone call or two for ten minutes every few days.

Betsy loved Liverpool, but, as I explained earlier, it didn't fulfil what she was looking for, because she still didn't know what she was looking for. She came home for a few weeks, then went travelling alone. Again, I went through the motions of her leaving, only this time her room remained more like her room, with all her trinkets, clothes and life possessions in it, and I knew that when she came home from travelling months later, she would be returning to me, even if that was temporary. Still, driving her to Heathrow to pop her on a plane to travel alone to

Bangkok felt enormous. And it was. We parents shouldn't diminish our emotions.

Betsy has been home since last summer now, but I know it is a short-term arrangement. She has just booked her flight for October 2024, and is saving as much as she can as quickly as she can so she can get back on a plane and travel to Thailand again, only this time she wants to get a working visa and stay abroad for a few years. Part of me hopes she does. I hope she finds her thing, her people.

I think the lesson I learned from Betsy leaving is that this is something I am going to go through time and time again. We have six babies who are going to grow up, and right now at least five can and will go on to live independently. Part of me is excited for that, especially on the days they're all tag-teaming Josh and me, or the house is a shithole, but part of me is dreading that empty nest. I know there will come a time when we will downsize our home because I don't want to walk past a load of empty shells each and every day. It's just such a huge change, isn't it? But parents survive when their kids move on. I know I'll be OK.

My parents

As much as my difficult and muddled upbringing has affected me in negative ways, I am determined that this pain and trauma will not bleed into how I parent my own children. Every day, I work hard to love, listen to and understand my children, and to learn what it is they need in that moment. I wish my mum and dad had done that for me, but they didn't – they couldn't. The lessons I have learned – and am still learning – about them, myself and the mother I want to be are invaluable. I have made changes and manifested a world for my family that is the polar opposite to the one in which I grew up. All the same, my parents and siblings have helped to shape the woman I've become, good and bad, and I acknowledge that here. In this section, I'll go through these different familial relationships, in the hope that my honesty will help you shed light on your own back story, and allow you to feel seen and heard – maybe for the first time.

♡

I am determined
that this pain
and trauma will
not bleed into
how I parent my
own children.

My dad

Once upon a time, I had a reading with an Irish psychic called Nadia. She was recommended to me by some of my followers, so I booked a meeting with her over Zoom. I told her I hadn't seen my dad for more than fourteen years and asked if she could explain why he doesn't see me, why he doesn't care about me, when he is one of the loveliest men you could meet. He will always chat to anyone; he is the type of guy who walks into a corner shop and chats to the assistant. He would go to work to fix a broken toilet and stay an extra half hour to chat to the lonely old lady he feels sorry for. I asked Nadia how it is that he seems able to live without me now when he was so much fun for so much of the time he was in my life. I didn't understand how he didn't miss me enough to make things right between us.

'He is a good man, but that's what you need to see: a man,' she said. 'He is a good man, whether he is speaking to a butcher, a baker, a lonely old lady or a little girl he once created. But just because he is a nice man who has good qualities, it doesn't mean he's a good *father*. That's a whole different ball game. You see, a good father couldn't live without his daughter for fourteen *days*, let alone fourteen years. Stop confusing what he is as a man with what he is as a father, because he isn't that; he hasn't ever really been that.'

And it just made sense. Here's what I knew from that day on:

Good people can be terrible parents.

This can make it harder for their children, as I found, as it reinforces the feeling that there is something wrong with us, and that's hard. It makes us carry the guilt and shame as if we're the ones in the wrong. But we're not.

Understanding this made everything easier for me – and I hope it helps you, too, if you're in a similar situation with a parent. It made the confusion I still had at that point disappear. The sadness I felt for myself was replaced with sadness for him, and my mum. I know that because of the way they did things with me, I have prioritised working on the family unit I have under my own roof, focusing on my relationship with my children and their relationships as siblings.

I will not repeat my parents' behaviour. I work hard to make my home safe for my kids, and I ensure they know they come above and before anything else.

Love oozes from our home. It's far from perfect, and it's loud and busy, but it's the most incredible place to be – and I believe the only reason it's like this is because of the lessons I learned from my parents and the negative feelings their choices gave me. I am beyond proud of how our family unit has looked for the past ten years. Now, I feel a sense of gratitude to my parents, because the choices they made when I was a child and a teenager, and how they made me feel, have given me the fire in my belly, a determination to be the best parent I can be.

My mum

I still see my mum regularly. The saying 'Time is a healer' is true, but I also think time helps you forget. My time with her now is nicer, better – because I am in a totally different place. I see her because I want to see her, not because I feel I need her. When she first landed back in my world after seeing her a few times a year for more than twenty years, I was in one of the worst places of my life. I was in the depths of an abusive relationship. My perpetrator had full control over who I was and wasn't allowed to see, and he decided that my mum was a 'safe' person. That meant I could see her as much as I liked. I imagine me just soaking her up, desperate for her love – desperate to have the mum I'd never had, for my girls to have a nan. It must have felt like a lottery win for her, after everything. But fast-forward ten years, I met the love of my life and the whole dynamic changed. I still wanted to see her, but in a way where it was no longer just me and her, it was no longer her trying to fix a desperately unhappy me. That must have been such a weird shift: for her to see me happy and loved, to see me in a relationship where I was cared for. I'm sure that, as pleased as she was for me, part of her was gutted at what she'd lost. See, parent–child relationships are always tricky, always in flux – even when the child is in her thirties.

I think my mum has accepted that the relationship between me and my siblings is done, it's over, so she no longer gets *as* upset about it. She comes over each week. I help her with sorting things she needs, and she organises my larder. It's not perfect, and a lot of the time I feel sad about the way things are, but it works, and it's the best our relationship has been for the last ten years.

We still don't talk about the heavy stuff. I don't even know if she's read any of my books. I tell her when I hit the *Sunday Times* bestseller list and she says, 'That's nice,' or 'Congratulations,' but then goes straight back to drinking her cup of tea, or telling me about what bulbs she's just planted on her roof garden, and that's it. It's so fucking weird because I think she's proud of me, I hope she's proud of me, but I don't really know. She's never told me she's proud of me, not once in my life. I can't imagine one of my kids being a bestselling author and me not shouting it from the rooftops. I'd tell them every day how proud I am of them, in the same way I tell Isaac I'm proud of him when he gets a week of merits and doesn't act like a dick at school; or when Betsy has a night out and sticks to her budget. I am proud of all my kids for all the big and little things.

I don't know how my mum feels about most things, because she just isn't a talker when it comes to her or us. Last week she came over and told me she felt down. It's the first time she's ever admitted it and, when I tried to delve, she said she hadn't seen my brothers on Mother's Day, or at all for months and it makes her sad. I told her she needs to tell them because they're probably so busy with their own lives they won't even realise she could be missing them or feeling low. However, she immediately refused – it wasn't up for a discussion. When she left, Josh and I spoke and he reminded me that my family looks how it does because no one in it talks or communicates their feelings, so nothing ever changes or gets resolved and it probably never will. That's why, within the family I've created, we talk about anything and everything. We communicate, we show emotion – any emotion and it's OK. It's not just accepted, it's encouraged: because I see the damage from not being able to do this from the family I was born into. My mum will talk to me for hours about stuff that doesn't focus on her, she will offer me advice on anything I have going on in my life, but she never discusses anything that is too close to home for the two of us. Maybe, deep down, she *is* super proud of me, maybe she's read all my books a hundred times and she thinks they're incredible but she just doesn't know how to show me or tell me that. That would be a shame, because I love hyping people up. I also love talking, sharing, understanding – even if it's about tricky situations, and even if I'm involved in those situations myself.

It would be my dream to sit with my mum and ask her questions. I want to know what her childhood looked like, her teenage years. I want her to tell me what the nightlife looked like in Manchester in the sixties. I want her to tell me all about meeting my dad: what he was like, if she ever loved him. But I also want to know all the deep stuff, the shit stuff. I want to ask her how she lived without me. How she walked out when I was the age Wilby is now and moved seven hours away from me. I want to ask her what she did every day for the twenty years we were apart. What did her days look like? What made her happy and what made her sad?

It hurts me that a part of me loves her so much, and yet another part has absolutely no clue who she is, what she thinks or how she feels. It's a huge headfuck when I delve into my childhood and I realise I don't have the balls to ask for these answers (which is partly why, unless I'm writing or journaling, I don't delve).

I accept Mum and I for who we are, and I just enjoy the relationship for what it is, because I'm mentally better off having a relationship with her than not. It's the best it's been for a very long time, and I have to take that as a win.

Parents are human

When we become adults, we see our parents for exactly what they are. We acquire this skill over the decades, learning to see everyone for who they really are and who they have always been, instead of what they or others want us to believe, but it can feel particularly strange when you begin to see your own parents in this light.

Think of your mum and dad, if you have been raised by them – and try this even if you haven't, or think about the people who did raise you. Take a minute or two now to just think about them as people: their personalities, their opinions and beliefs, the way they treat others, the things they said to you growing up, the way they put you to bed and woke you up. I know my mum's strengths, I know her faults, and it's the same for my dad. And I'm sure that when you think about your parents, properly study them, you'll find the same thing is true for you. You can learn a lot from looking back at their relationship: the realities of how hard things can be, and how even good people can do or say bad things sometimes.

It doesn't matter what you were told as a child, or who was telling you it; right now, as an adult looking back, you know what kind of parents you have or had. You will be aware of stuff they've done that perhaps wasn't great, perhaps was terrible. Some of you reading this may have had the opposite; you may have had the most incredible, supportive and loving parents who always put you first. What I've learned as I've grown older is that whatever our parents were like, as adults, we can understand our time with them better. Did you feel safe and loved no matter what, or did you have that feeling in your tummy where something just wasn't right? Now, when you look back, do you love them unconditionally, because even when they got it wrong, you know they were trying to get it right, or are you aware they just weren't great people or good parents?

Remember this when you're raising your own children: they won't always be tiny. They won't be able to be manipulated, lied to or be used as pawns in someone else's game. They will see everything one day, from who said what about whom, to which people felt safe to them, and whose needs were prioritised – and that's what you need to remember. What's tough now won't be tough forever. What they believe and see right now won't look like this when they have grown and have more life experience.

Breaking generational patterns

This is why we need to try and be the best versions of ourselves, and that doesn't mean being perfect – it just means always trying to put their needs above our own, and parking our hate for other people in front of them. Their little eyes are watching everything we do, and their little ears soak up everything they hear us say. When we can't be the best versions of ourselves, we need to own that, we have to take responsibility – explain why we did the things we did, or said the things we said – and we have to apologise. It's OK to not always get it right, but for a child to learn right from wrong, the adults around them need to acknowledge it and attempt to make things better. This is how the world will make sense to them; it's how they will grow into decent human beings, and it teaches them the most important skills for getting through in life: communication and honesty.

The sad part for so many of us, me included, is that we parent well *because* of our own shit childhoods. As I explained earlier, I don't think about how to parent based on how well my parents did it, because my parents made some catastrophically shit decisions that led to a childhood full of confusion, pain and trauma. I parent my children the way I *wasn't* parented after my mum disappeared, and I do everything in my power to ensure they never feel the way I did. The thought of any of my kids questioning their worth because they feel they're not good enough for me, that they're not loved by me, makes my brain ache and my heart hurt. I cannot bear the thought of them ever falling asleep with those overwhelming feelings of abandonment and rejection, or questioning my love for them, and I cannot cope with the thought of them ever not being able to talk to me.

I parent the way I do because I was failed: that's the top and bottom of it. I don't think I was failed because my parents are bad people – they're not. My dad is one of the funniest men you'll ever meet. He's honest and genuine, and he would give a hitchhiker a lift anywhere in the world to get them to their destination, while being fully invested in their story. My mum has worked her arse off her whole life, she's never forgotten a family member's birthday, and she has made any house she's lived in feel like a home to anyone who enters it – and she makes the best egg in a cup in history. They are both good people.

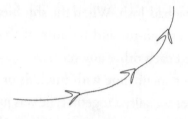

My siblings

My three siblings all see each other, and I think they've all started seeing my dad again since he had a health scare over a year ago. They spend their Christmases together, but I'm no longer a part of it. I have mentioned in previous books that I don't speak to my siblings, and I kind of left it there, but I know many of you want to know why.

My oldest brother

I wrote in my first book how my oldest brother was my hero. He has always been my other brother's hero, and right now he's playing hero to my sister and her son. I truly believe he never had children because, when our parents divorced, he was the only adult child, and he spent his young life picking up the pieces and making things OK for his three baby siblings. For the first thirty years of my life, he was my go-to whenever the shit hit the fan, but since 2014, I've had Josh. When the shit hits the fan now, I have a different go-to, and because of that, I think we just didn't need each other any more.

He has never spent time with my kids or in my home, and we've never socialised together; he was just there when I needed him. I've often questioned if I was the bad person because of that, but the reality is I think it's probably been a relief for him that I have someone else to care for me the first time in my life. I can imagine it was relentless and draining for him having to look after everyone. I would hang out with him now, but it's not something we ever really did back then when we were in touch, and I think he would much rather sit in front of the TV with his wife or go to the pub after work with the lads.

Two years ago, Mum and I were looking through a huge box of her old photos. I don't have any photos of me as a little girl, or of my mum and dad. I brought three photos home to show Josh, as I looked so much like Wilby in them and I posted one online. Within an hour, I got a message from my eldest brother asking me to return the photo to Mum's because my sister wanted them all 'kept together', as she was planning to make an album. My tummy did a flip at his message. I replied and pointed out to him that I found his message odd because he's not on social media, so I wasn't sure how he'd seen my post – and then I asked, if he *was* on social media, why he hadn't congratulated me on my second bestselling book, about which I'd recently posted on my channels. He replied saying he thought it was best we spoke face to face, as it was clear I had 'issues about things'. I decided not to reply.

A few months later, Mum told me my brother hadn't been able to work for a while, so I sent him a message offering to gift him some money that would cover his mortgage and bills and see him straight for a while, as he always had done the same for me. He didn't reply to my text despite it delivering, so I sent the same message on WhatsApp and it double blue-ticked within minutes, showing he'd read it. He never replied. That was over two years ago, and I haven't seen or spoken to him since.

This is another elephant in the room between me and my mum. She never mentioned the three photos I posted through her door. She just came round a few days later, as normal – and we've never discussed the fact that my eldest brother hasn't spoken to me since. It's just been accepted, never questioned. It's so different to the way I manage things under my own roof, the way I encourage my kids and husband to talk, shout, think and question everything, anything. But it also reminds me that this is the way we were all raised, and it's how my siblings continue to live. It's their normal. I'm the one who has changed, I'm the one who does the opposite of everything that was forced upon us for a huge part of our lives – so maybe that makes me the black sheep of the family.

My sister

I haven't had any contact with my sister for more than six years. It was over my first book. I had written nothing but nice things about her, but she didn't agree. Because of a sentence at the end of one paragraph, she was unhappy and emailed my publishers in February 2018. She ended the email by stating that she also would not be providing any confirmation that the content of the rest of the book was true as she had previously planned to do. Because of that, my mum also decided she was no longer going to confirm to the publisher that she supported the book. I called my eldest brother in shock; I told him I was just going to remove any mention of my sister in the book.

So I wrote her out of the book – and my life.

She's not my person, because I am not hers. I feel she blames me for why our family ended up looking like it did, and I don't have the strength, energy or time to try and convince her otherwise. And actually, I don't want to.

Today, I have to prioritise who is right and wrong for me, and I know, deep down, she's never been right for me so I am not right for her. We don't have to stay in touch with family members who make us feel like shit and we don't have to explain ourselves to people who choose not to get it. We need to do whatever we can to look after ourselves, to prioritise staying well and be around the family we have created for ourselves as adults, whatever that looks like.

My other brother

I haven't spoken to my other brother since I blocked him on everything on 10 May 2020. There was no big explosion, just a build-up over a long period of time. I believe, as adults, we get to an age where we have to take some responsibility and seek help when our actions break other people, but I felt he was never prepared to do that. It wasn't something I could raise with him either. So, in the end, four years ago, I made the choice to walk away from him.

I think, in a way, it felt easier for him to not have me around. It's much easier to cut out those who are going to pull you and challenge you on certain things. Occasionally, I really miss him. He's probably the one I miss the most, because the majority of the time he was my best friend. I don't think there's anyone else in the world that can make me laugh like he could but he's also a really complex character. I think, deep down, he wanted out from what our relationship was as siblings and, like I said with my sister, I have to accept that and just hope he goes on in life to be an amazing human and do incredible things. That's in him; it's just that, at times, he struggles to see it.

The lessons I've learned from my siblings

- ❤ Blood isn't always thicker than water.
- ❤ My brothers and sister are not my people. And I'm learning to accept it.
- ❤ Although, biologically, we were born to the same parents, our upbringing and experiences were totally different to each other. Despite us being siblings, our childhoods were a million miles apart.
- ❤ Sometimes, those who should want you to succeed and be happy, don't.
- ❤ These people, family or otherwise, don't deserve your love, time or attention. Move on with grace.

I'm not sad that I don't fit in with my siblings anymore. I no longer wish I was a part of their lives, and when I FaceTime Mum on Christmas Day and they're all in the background eating dinner together, I don't feel like I'm missing out. I feel relieved that I'm not trying to fit in, desperately trying to belong to something I've never really felt a part of.

These days, I look at the family I was born into as just a temporary thing. It was to teach me, to break me, to heal me, but most importantly to show me what family should look like. It showed me the importance of raising my babies as siblings, even if they don't share the same biological parents. It taught me that I never want anyone in my home to look around and think, 'I don't fit in here.'

And who knows? Maybe one day it could all go wrong. Maybe *I'm* wrong. But for now, just as they have for the past ten years, the six children I've raised under my roof blow me away constantly with the love and loyalty they show one another, and the weird and unique relationships they share. I hope that I've done enough to keep those relationships strong enough to last a lifetime, to continue long after I've gone. I hope that if they have kids, those kids can enjoy being cousins, and that my six can be the aunties and uncles they and I never had for their siblings' kids. I hope I've broken that generational trauma. I hope I've instilled into them what a loving family looks like. Being a healthy family is hard work, but goodness me, it's worth it. I genuinely believe that, as a mother, what I've created under my roof is my greatest achievement to date.

PART III: RELATIONSHIPS – LOVING YOURSELF SO YOU CAN LOVE OTHERS

As you will appreciate from reading this book so far, and from following my work online and in my community, the path of true love has not run smooth for me. Managing ex-partners can be as tricky as managing teens, and we've already established how tricky that can be!

One universal truth, when it comes to working out your romantic make-ups and break-ups, is that, when children are involved, they really need to come first. My parents' divorce and their subsequent parenting (or anti-parenting) of me really highlights this – as does the fallout from Josh's past broken relationships and my own. In this section, I'll share my stories in the hope that you can connect with parts of them, and take some ideas or tools with you as you navigate your own way forward.

How to co-parent

One of the questions I get asked most frequently – in comments, in private messages and at the centre – is: 'How do I co-parent with my ex?'

In an ideal world, everyone would prioritise their children after a break-up and find a way to be amicable with their ex and their new partner, and they'd all co-parent in harmony with no drama. But this isn't an ideal world, and it's rare to separate from the parent of your children and find that everything bobs along with everyone feeling happy and harmonious all the time.

What I will say is that it all comes down to whether your ex-partner is a perpetrator of domestic abuse (be it mental, physical, sexual or financial).

If they are not, you will be able to co-parent amicably in time. It may take time, but you will get there. Truly. Hang on in there.

If they are, you will never co-parent amicably, and your

future will be about managing the relationship to the best of your ability, while protecting your own mental health and that of your children as much as you can.

I have three daughters by two ex-partners: one is a perpetrator, and one isn't. Don't get me wrong, the first few years of trying to navigate things for my youngest daughter (whose dad isn't a perpetrator) were still tough. There were things said and done, and public Facebook statuses were written that felt overwhelmingly devastating. I genuinely couldn't ever see it getting better, but we had a baby who was less than six months old, and we had no choice but to co-parent. Over time, things became better, and now I know he knows our daughter is safe and loved when she's in my care, and I know it's the same when she spends her time with him in his house. We parent totally differently, our households aren't run in the same way, but we respect that Edie has two lives where she is cared for at both homes – and it works.

Now let's go back to my separation with my eldest girls' dad. I attempted to co-parent with him for eight years after we fled him and our family home. When we 'got on', it was almost harder, because it wasn't genuine. I knew it wouldn't last, and it worsened my anxiety more than when he was calling me a 'stupid cunt' in a text message, or screaming down the phone in front of the girls that he wanted me dead because I'd sent them in the wrong coats or shoes for their day out with him.

It was hell. And it was so wrong that I had to do it.

I know from my own experience, and from stories shared with me by the women we support each day, that handing over your children to your perpetrator is one of the times they are most likely to abuse you – even if it's in a Sainsbury's car park at 4.30pm on a Sunday afternoon. It's wrong that family courts don't have centres in every area for domestic abuse survivors to do free handovers without question or having to provide evidence of abuse. Sure, there are 'agencies' set up to do handovers, depending on where you live, but they charge – *a lot* – and they don't always do the times you require. As part of a court order, I believe it should be already arranged that the handover should take place in a safe space, with safe support. Our babies are the most precious things to us, and having to hand over your children to your abuser is one of the most terrifying things in this world. It destroys lives. It allows the abuse to continue, and it doesn't protect you or your children – which, ironically, is what the family court is there to do. It's criminal.

Lessons I've learned the hard way

Something I recommend to the women we work with at the centre is to have a separate phone for their perpetrator. So, if you are in this situation (or know someone who is), change the number (if the perpetrator has it) of the original phone that you use daily, then get a second (basic burner) phone (£25 on eBay) and a pay-as-you-go SIM.

Then give the second number to the perpetrator – literally just send a text saying, 'This is my new number.' (And if they *did* have the old number, that's been changed anyway, so it's now gone altogether.)

This means you've instantly taken back some control without them even being aware of it. You now have a phone that's just for them. At first, the women we support generally believe that they have to answer every call and text they receive from their perpetrator. They then over-think how they should respond when he texts – in case they 'show someone', as they've threatened to for years.

We educate them on why they behave like this. It all comes down to the perpetrators trying to exert the maximum level of power and control over them, even when the relationship has ended.

Here's how to take back your phone power:

- ♥ If there is a court order in place where your children need to have phone calls with your ex throughout the week, you can turn the phone on at these times, then turn it off again straight after.
- ♥ You can decide if and when you look at the phone. Some of the women we support check it each day at a certain time; others leave it off for days at a time.
- ♥ Your ex-partner does not need to have access to you freely just because you've had children with them. This is one of the biggest things women think they will 'get into

trouble' for. When they say this out loud, I ask, 'Who did you think you will be in trouble with?' And they don't even know – it's just been drilled into them by the perpetrator that they have to have access to them, and that if the survivor goes against this, there will be a problem.

Another personal lesson I've learned from all those years of post-separation abuse is that it's best not to reply, no matter how much you want to. I saw an Instagram reel a lady made the other day where she was looking at a message on her phone, making all these different facial expressions, and the caption read, 'Just trying to work out which version of me is going to reply – healed me or petty me.' It made me laugh, because all those years ago, I used to receive so many text messages from the girls' dad, and Josh would get them from the boys' mum. The messages would hit my screen and, at first, they would look quite short, but each time at the bottom right of the screen, it said, 'READ MORE,' and when I clicked that, it would open a message that was about the length of this chapter! Honestly, the sheer shit spewed at me continuously, day in, day out, made me feel so unwell. I would read it all, over and over, to somehow try and digest it. I would rage, cry, feel the injustice of his words. I would feel sad my babies had to be around someone who was capable of writing so much vitriol towards their mum, and I would spend my night going back and forward, sending lengthy messages to him trying to explain my side in an attempt to make him see how abusive he was.

It was pointless. Trying to make him see reason was hopeless, it was like talking to a brick wall, so I had to focus on what I could control: my actions. I look back now and think he would never have taken in the content of my messages; he probably didn't even read my responses. He would never have seen my side of the argument he'd started, nor would he have recognised his own behaviours as abusive. I wasted so much time on it; if I added up all those minutes of reading his messages, then texting back lengthy replies, it would come to hours, if not days, over the years I spent doing it. All that time I wasted trying to reason with a narcissist, an abuser, could have been spent cleaning the windows or vacuuming – and that would be the only time it would have made sense to prioritise those crap jobs!

Wait: A lesson in calm from Josh

Josh always used to say to me, 'Give it twenty-four hours.' It's the same rule we have now with the trolls when they hit us hard and heavy. Sit on it, give it a day, and if I still feel the same the following day, then I can go back. After we put that rule in place, I rarely replied, and I rarely do now with the trolls. Those initial feelings, that urge to go back and have your say, to prove your point, whip out the evidence and question them on their revolting behaviour, usually subside within a few hours, and within twenty-four, you give no fucks, because you see it's all just about them. His messages were nothing to do with me, and it's the same with the trolls now. It was all down to his own issues and anger that he was projecting on to me because he was so mad about weird, random stuff, like having to care for his own daughters.

In the end, I stopped replying. I totally ignored him, or I thumbsed-up his lengthy messages where he ripped apart my parenting, called me every insult he could think of, slagged off my husband and sons, and threw everything else he wanted to at me.

Please take on board what I've written here. When you have a device that your ex-perpetrator can contact you on day or night, your anxiety will forever be in a heightened state, because they will have access to you 24/7. You won't know when they might text or call, what they might say, what their state of mind might be, where you stand. Having a mobile phone just for them that you have the power to turn off and leave in a drawer means you're stopping that access to you, and you're choosing when to view the odd bit of shit they send. It might also mean they give up quicker, because they live for the reaction; they want the fight, the text war. When they fire off a message that doesn't get a reaction, then follow it up with a phone call and find themselves met with your voicemail, they're not getting that instant hit they're used to, the one they desperately need in that moment, the one that they crave. But

♡

Nobody who
makes us feel
like shit should
have unlimited
access to us.

ultimately, that's not the point. This is about making *you* feel better – because nobody who makes us feel like shit should have unlimited access to us, even if we created a child with them.

Every break-up is hard ... accept it

Breaking up is hard to do. You can separate from a decent partner, and things will still feel tough. I don't know anyone in my whole life who has split up with or divorced their partner without any heartache at all, no matter what they tell people or how they make it look in an Instagram post or story. It's OK to do the 'second phone' thing with an ex who isn't a perpetrator too, until the feelings of hurt and upset lessen, until things feel more settled and make a bit more sense. We absolutely have to do what's best for us in order to get through situations that seem set to destroy us. So, I am here to remind you to put yourself first for once, and to reclaim your power over your own thoughts and actions. You can do it, I promise.

When any woman I've advised the 'second phone' tactic to has actually done it, the improvement to their lives and mental health has been instant – and in the days and weeks that follow, when it sets in that they absolutely can have boundaries in place, and they don't have to make themselves constantly available to their ex, they're often left in a state of shock that they didn't do this sooner, that they didn't know they could, that they didn't realise they were 'allowed to'. It's such a simple thing to do, yet sometimes things that are so obvious and easy to implement seem invisible to us, because we're so busy wading through the trenches, trying to survive each day. Whether you adopt this tactic to protect you from nasty messages, voicemails and constant calls from a perpetrator, or because you are experiencing the physical heartache and turmoil of a separation from a non-abusive partner, it's vital that you do what you can to protect yourself and your children as you're getting through it.

Co-parenting: getting on the same wavelength

Edie likes it when something happens and I talk to her dad or his girlfriend to work a way out going forward that we're all involved with. When I hang up the phone, she asks me things like, 'Do you like them, Mum?' and 'Do you think they're nice?' I always reassure her that I like them and that we get on (even when we don't!), and I see her physically relax at that response.

I know from Edie that she is at her happiest when she thinks her dad and I are friends. It's a question she asks me regularly. In fact, she asks me many questions regularly for reassurance on how I feel about her dad, and I know she does the same with him, because she will often tell me stories of things he and I did together when we were younger that he's clearly told her. Her whole face lights up when she recounts a funny tale to me, and she's eager to

Put yourself first for once, and reclaim your power over your own thoughts and actions.

hear my side. When I tell her the same funny stories, or new ones, of things we got up to when we were at school, she cries with laughter – she has the best giggle. She gets me to tell her the same stories over and over, and she cries with laughter. I have a school photo of the two of us in year seven when we were just eleven, and she loves looking at it. Our relationship was how she began; it's part of her history. Even when you're not together with your ex, if they haven't been abusive you shouldn't take that away from a child. Your past love is their origin story.

Finding the strength to leave an abusive relationship

I saw an article was shared on Instagram recently about women 'staying' in abusive relationships with their children. The comments section was full of the usual questions of 'Why doesn't she leave?', and there were also a lot of voices chiming in on how stupid we are to stay.

For the record, a victim of domestic abuse is never stupid. I was at my absolute smartest when I spent a decade in an abusive relationship. I was on high alert every hour of every day, even during the good times – sometimes more so during the good times, because I knew that it could change in a split second into a bad time. I was constantly planning, checking, ensuring he had nothing to get angry about or lose it over. Everything I did back then was to protect my girls. When things were bad, I did everything in my power to make them better as quickly as possible – again, I was forever thinking, planning. So no, people who live with domestic abuse aren't stupid – they're clever. They have to be able to think in situations of immense stress and pressure, and they have to act as if nothing's wrong to the whole world while living with constant trauma. There's absolutely nothing stupid about us.

Children hate conflict between adults – and if they don't, that's even more worrying, because they should. By the time I fled the girls' dad, Betsy and Lula could sit and watch a film or play a game while the shouting, screaming and stuff being smashed went on around them, and they wouldn't flinch. Betsy knew only to comfort me when he wasn't there. When he was around, she knew to ignore me, no matter what state I was in. They learned how to stay safe really quickly, which is terrifying to think about.

When we left their dad, Betsy was six and Lula wasn't even two. At the same time, I was being called in to Betsy's school, because she wasn't being kind to other kids, and when she was being spoken to about it, she showed no remorse and continued. She remembers being that kid to this day. That's what happens when children aren't bothered about conflict between adults; the devastating impact on their behaviour can be seen even when they're tiny . . .

When I left with the girls, we had to do a lot of work to change things, and to teach Betsy especially that so much of what had been her 'normal' was wrong. Was sick. I can't count the apologies I made to them both – and still, over a decade later – for what they didn't just witness, but also endured, every single day, from when they were growing inside me until the day they decided they couldn't see him anymore, years after I left. I can't describe the physical pain my heart has felt at points when writing this chapter at the trauma the three of us still carry from him, from that. It wrecks me.

I'll repeat what I said before: in an ideal world, everyone would prioritise their children after a break-up and be amicable with their ex, their new partner, and we would all co-parent in harmony, and there would be no drama. If you've managed to do this, then congratulations to you, that's incredible – but most of us haven't, because most of the time when we divorce or separate, hearts get broken, people you once loved become unrecognisable, and that makes you lose trust in the world. Feelings and emotions feel impossible to manage, and you find yourself entering a brand new, unknown world with your babies, which can be just brutal to manage some days. So, if you're there, and you're finding it difficult, I hope some of this chapter helps you to get through a really tough time. It might feel like it's lasting a lifetime, but I promise it doesn't – it will actually go by far quicker than you imagine. I will cover some more about leaving an abusive relationship later in the book and I hope this somehow makes you feel less alone.

Trauma teaches us empathy

In the last few years, since opening the women's centre and seeing the way some women and children live daily, I have realised something. I have met and been around so many men and women born into loving homes with parents who have stayed together their whole lives and raised them in a perfect bubble. And you know what's weird? I sometimes look at those adults and feel sad for them, because not only are they totally oblivious to how other people have to live, but they also have absolutely zero interest in helping, supporting or understanding them – or, in fact, anyone other than the people perfect enough to already be inside their perfect bubbles with them.

Many of these 'bubble' children grow and evolve into some of the most judgemental adults you could ever meet. Do you know the types of people I'm referring to? If you asked one of these people about their childhood, they'd tell you it was perfect – and to them, it was. Their parents, and probably their grandparents, and their aunts and uncles, and anyone else who was involved in that childhood would agree . . . But that perfection means they've never experienced the things so many of us come across every single day. They know nothing about domestic abuse, addiction and poverty. They've never struggled financially, or been in any kind of situation where they question whether they'll physically survive the heartbreak.

I used to feel envious of these kinds of people, both as a child, when I walked into their homes and saw the love and often wealth that poured from their surroundings, and as an adult. Years ago, I was envious of the people I knew who had breezed through life without any real worries or issues, because I'd never had that, and then I'd felt guilty that when I became a mum, my children didn't have that from me – I didn't give them a 'perfect life' like the one so many people take for granted. But when I sit and think about it, I wouldn't want a life like that, and I wouldn't want my children to have one like it either, because so many people you meet in life will need you to offer help and understanding without judgement. In order to have fire in your belly for something, to raise awareness for it, you have to understand it, properly *get* it – you need to know all the gory details, and the difference between the facts and the myths. You have to be ready to defend it against society's assumptions, and you have to accept knowing things might not get better in your lifetime, but it's still worth fighting for change.

The reality is, when you have that fire in your belly, and you go on to support people in dire situations, seeing them go from the lowest lows to shining bright, there is no better feeling in the world. My children understand domestic abuse; some of them have lived through it. All of them, bar the youngest two (Wilby because we weren't 'there' when he was born, and Edie because she was too tiny to remember), lived with us when we lived in poverty. Some days, without Josh's mum supporting us, we wouldn't have eaten, because despite us both working and trying our best, we were financially ruined for the first few years we were together. I want my kids to remember those feelings. I want Isaac and Lula to feel fortunate they can go on the skiing trips we couldn't afford for Betsy and Seb. And I also want them to be able to spot the kids who can't afford to go, and not look down on them, because we've been there too.

And that's the thing with life: we could be back there again one day. Who knows? I believe that even if you have a happy marriage, a supportive family and wealth, you should absolutely educate yourself and your children on the sheer shit other people endure and live through, often through no fault of their own. The world is never going to become a better place if we only look after our own. I know so many people locally who have a vast amount of wealth – millions of pounds in the bank (I'm related to some of them) – and they look down on anyone who they judge as not doing well in life. These people will never tip their hairdresser, even though she's given them the most amazing cut and colour; nor will they the waitress who served them, even though they got five-star service and an incredible meal. And not only would they not donate to a local charity, they also wouldn't even bother to find out what it's all about.

I hope that if some of these people came and hung out in our centre for the day, they'd want to spend more time there, because my team and the women and children we support are amazing. I hope they would feel the joy of what we do, and they would go away and change their views on the world, and they would then pass this on to their children. Yet, unfortunately, many wealthy people who have time on their hands and the power to make such changes to this world could spend a day in my women's centre and still not get it. They'd go home and look at their own children, and think they're right to shield them from us, from what we do. They think that by raising their kids in this perfect bubble, they're doing the right thing. Maybe I'm the one who's got it wrong, but the way I look at it is: the world isn't a perfect bubble, and one day they're going to come across stuff that they have no experience or awareness of, and they are not going to know where to start in coping with it.

Sobering statistics

Here are the latest stats I can find about the way people are living today:

♡

The world is never
going to become
a better place
if we only look
after our own.

- More than one in five people in the UK live in poverty (Joseph Rowntree foundation)
- One in five people aged over sixteen in the UK have experienced domestic abuse (fearfree.org.uk)
- One in five children in every class (when they start school) will have been living with domestic abuse since they were born. Normal class sizes in our country are around thirty children; that means at least six children in your child's class have been living with domestic abuse since they came into this world (SaveLives)

It is our absolute duty to educate ourselves and our children on the devastating things happening in our world, because every single one of us, at some point, is going to come into contact with someone who needs us to understand them. Shouldn't we all want our children to be able to recognise someone who is in a vulnerable position, or less fortunate than them? If you are in a position to raise your children in a safe, warm and loving home, and you have no financial worries, surely it can only be a positive thing for them to be aware of the other children who don't have these luxuries?

I look at our eldest five children: the boys have lived with addiction and parental alienation. Seb had to be video interviewed at Torquay police station during family court proceedings. Our two eldest girls lived with domestic abuse. We all then lived in poverty. Edie has experienced so many emotional issues because adults around her weren't grown-up or child-focused enough in her dad's family to let her feel nothing but love after we separated. She also lived with Josh and me at a time when we had no money and were in a huge amount of debt. That's five children who have all had experiences I wouldn't wish for . . . then along comes Wilby. Josh and I, his parents, are still together and in love. Financially, we are in a much better position. He has five elder siblings who dote on him, and he is surrounded by all the things I spoke about earlier. He pretty much has all the same advantages as the child being raised in those 'perfect bubble' families. The difference is that Wilby will be raised with the awareness that his siblings' lives haven't always looked like this, and he will also continue to come to the women's centre, as all my kids have, where he will learn about the incredible people it is there to support.

I've seen how sharing this knowledge helps those who feel isolated and alone to grow and get healthy. It sounds simple, but it can make so much difference. And when I hear stories about what families are going through, whether at the centre, on my page, or from my children, who are seeing and hearing stuff at school, I know we still need to make a lot of changes as a society.

Moving on and moving up

A few months ago, I did a podcast with Betsy, and on the way back she said, 'Let's dance.' She put on a song at full volume that means *everything* to both of us, and we drove along, dancing in our seats and singing at the tops of our voices, smiling at each other. The thing that made me feel such overwhelming joy in that moment was the contrast between what that song felt like then, that day in the car, and what it felt like when we first played it. The song was Alesha Dixon's 'The Boy Does Nothing'.

We first heard that song in the car on the way to soft play when she was a toddler. It was just us two in the car. She had watched me clean the house after her dad had smashed it up. He'd thrown a box of dry cereal across the kitchen, then kicked the dog because Stewie the rabbit (who lived between the house and garden, depending on his mood) had eaten through our telephone wire. He would have kicked the rabbit if he could have, but I was one step ahead (like I explained earlier, I was always one step ahead), so I'd already popped Stewie outside and he was long gone, burrowed under the decking as if he knew he was in the shit for chewing through the phone wire. So instead it was the poor dog got who got a kick before he stormed out of the house.

Betsy was sitting on the sofa watching *Lazy Town*, while I was on my knees, cleaning up his mess and looking at the dog's sad and puzzled face, consumed with desperation. I wish I could explain the feelings you get when abuse is being perpetrated on you. During those ten years, I felt things I'd never felt before, and have never felt after. Sometimes I would be so desperately sad that I couldn't stop the tears. I would wail, like an injured cat, because I didn't know how to make it stop, and I hated that it was happening. Sometimes I would beg like a child for him to stop. Other times, I would feel this underlying rage, like a hot flush that consumed my entire being. I would hear my heart pounding in my ears, feel the vomit rise up to my throat then settle back to my tummy, and I would imagine all sorts of ways I could get out of the relationship. I'd pray he would leave me for someone else. I would picture a physical fight he would start between us where I could act in self-defence and kill him, leaving me and the girls to finally be free. I would feel such shame for thinking those things when we were back in the honeymoon period, and then I'd worry that my wish that he would leave me for another woman would actually come true. It was so fucked.

It's not you, its him

When I was trapped in an abusive relationship, I hated myself. The feeling that caused me the most distress was when I was consumed with anger at myself:

- Anger that I had got involved with him in the first place
- Anger about what my daughters were experiencing
- Anger at the way I allowed him to treat us
- Anger that I didn't fight back
- Anger that I *did* fight back
- Anger that I was weak
- Anger that I was as bad as him
- Anger at the feeling of being trapped with him
- Anger that we might never break free, and this might be how I would live until the day I died

That anger towards myself caused a deep rage that makes me feel sick to this day. Sometimes, I would feel it all day, every day; sometimes weekly; and at other times I could go months without feeling it. It just depended on what he was doing at that time. I would lose it. The only way I can describe it is that I would attempt to beat myself to death. Even as I'm writing this, my eyes are stinging, the lump in my throat is painful, and I have the feeling of pin pricks on both my arms and down my spine. It makes me realise there is so much I've still buried in order to survive. I wish

I could have shaken myself and convinced myself that it wasn't me, it was him. It was all his fault. But I didn't. Instead, I literally beat myself up in anger at myself.

These deep depths of self-loathing would usually start when he was verbally abusive to me and he wouldn't stop, or when he was gearing up, getting ready to go. I know I did it to show him I didn't care what happened to me; it was almost as if I thought that if he believed I had no self-worth, he wouldn't bother targeting me. The reality is, I had never had any self-worth. I would start by pulling at my hair, until I ripped out whole clumps. When I saw the hair leave my head, I felt brief relief, despite the way my scalp would be throbbing, but it was never enough. I would punch myself, always in the sides or top of my head. I would run into the wall at the top of the stairs (I could get a decent run-up from our bedroom, so when I slammed into it, I could feel the pain rush down my body). I would run my arms under water that was so hot it scalded me. I would do a backwards head-butt so I could feel the huge lump and excruciating pain, but no one else could see it. Most of my injuries remained invisible to the outside world. See, once again, abuse victims are clever – always thinking ahead, even when we are at our very worst.

When I think back, I must have looked possessed. I would scream the weirdest, craziest stuff. I think by that point I was in total meltdown. I felt so crazy. I wanted him to believe that I *was* crazy; maybe so he would leave me, or maybe just so he would stop. Only once did he hold me until I stopped, after I'd torn out a lot of hair and sliced my shoulder open on the corner of our bedroom drawers. There was blood everywhere. It wasn't a nice hold; as he held me, he still whispered in my ear that I was fucking nuts, and reminded me if I left, Betsy would stay with him because of this kind of mental behaviour. Gradually, my anger turned to sobs, and then he left me in a heap on our bed, cringing with embarrassment and feeling like I was insane and didn't deserve to be a mum. On all the other occasions when he witnessed me react to him like this, he would say the same cruel things, but then he would laugh at me and walk out, leaving me at my very worst, and leaving me even more determined to beat myself to death.

Flashbacks to fear – and helping myself

I've had two of those incidents in the time I've been with Josh. I have never told anyone else about them other than my therapist, and writing this here for thousands of people to read feels pretty frightening. It's not something I'm proud of, but I've come to realise that I'll forever be healing, and that this is my reality, my truth.

The first one was in 2014, and the last was in December 2021. Another one started a few months ago, but I managed to calm myself before I got there. Little wins.

Both times, it happened over really trivial things, but escalated because I was trying to explain my point, but Josh's mind was already made up, and he wouldn't meet me in the middle. I felt like he wasn't listening to me when I knew my points were valid. I also felt he was controlling the argument; my rational brain knows he wasn't, but when I'm feeling those emotions, it takes me back to my ex, to us, and ultimately to how I ended up behaving during those arguments.

In 2014, we'd been on a night out and I was really pissed. We had only just got together, and I hadn't, at that point, begun to understand or learn about the behaviours I'd displayed for a decade with my ex. At that time in my life, I didn't even know reactive abuse – when the perpetrator of abuse deliberately triggers their partner into reacting to the abuse *aggressively* – was a thing. In 2021, it happened at a time when I was feeling really unwell mentally. I had too much on, both work-wise and at home, and an argument that in hindsight could have been resolved really easily ended up turning into hell on earth. Not only would Josh not listen to what I was saying, he stormed out of our room and went downstairs. All those unjust feelings arose in seconds, and the day ended with me smashing holes in our bedroom walls with a metal bookend, ripping my hair out, then beating the shit out of my own head and backwards head-butting my chest of drawers. The difference, during both of those incidents, is that when Josh heard me losing it, when he walked back into the room to see me behaving like that, he did everything in his power to calm me down and make it stop. He held me; he reminded me how to regulate my breathing as I descended into panic attacks both times; he held a paper bag to my face; he stroked my hair and reassured me repeatedly.

The day after the last incident, I dressed as an elf and delivered presents all over Torbay for the women's centre. To look at the pictures and videos from that day, anyone would have thought I was in a good place. An amazing place. It was just before Christmas, and any of you watching me on social media would have thought my life looked rosy. But our marriage felt like it was crumbling around me, and the guilt and self-loathing I held for myself was really devastating – all because of a stupid argument over nothing, that had led to one of my worst-ever self-harm incidents. Here I was, battered and bruised, with bald patches on my head, and my bedroom was now covered in holes and smashed glass. The shame and embarrassment I continued to feel was horrific, and it just wasn't going. Every time I looked at Josh, I teared up again.

And so, I realised I needed help. I needed to *not* bury these feelings and just hope they never reared their heads again. I booked therapy, then told my therapist what had happened. I also told her about all the times I'd done this throughout my ten-year relationship, and I explained that I was frightened I'd never stop feeling these rages. I told her they made me question who I was as a person.

She reminded me of some key things I want you to remember if you ever feel a similar sense of self-loathing or experience self-harming episodes. She reminded me that I had gone seven years without one incident like this. Yes, to me, seven years was not long enough, but it was substantial. She couldn't guarantee that I'd never get to this point again in my lifetime, but we discussed why it had started, what my triggers were. She helped me see that I was once a nineteen-year-old girl, already damaged, already angry at so many people and full of trauma, who had met a man who literally drove her insane for a decade.

His goal was to make me crazy, to make me believe I was crazy, so I was totally dependent and reliant upon him. Ten years of that is a fucking long time, especially at the tender age of nineteen, when my whole world should have been starting. When I left that relationship, I never sought help because of the shame I felt, because he spent so much of his time after I left telling everyone around us that I was just as bad as him. I chose to pretend it didn't happen, and I convinced myself it would never happen again.

My therapist and I spoke about coping mechanisms and how to communicate if I feel those feelings beginning inside me. I think it has worked. Every day now, I practise the toolkit we worked on together. I do breathing exercises every day, I use the tapping technique she taught me whenever I feel anxious or stressed, and I communicate my feelings. As I mentioned, only once since 2021 have I felt that sense of brewing self-loathing after an argument, and I recognised immediately that my brain was taking me back to that relationship, where it was unsafe. So, I said out loud to Josh that I was feeling those feelings. I asked him to leave our room, and he did. I tapped, breathed, and whispered repeatedly that I was safe, then cried like a baby for a good ten minutes until my body ran out of tears and ached from the sobs. Josh then came back into the room, scooped me into his arms and just held me. We sat and finished the argument as a discussion instead. It was a lesson for us both, and showed me that I can control how I act, no matter what my brain has tried to trick me into believing. I was about to automatically revert to what I'd known for so long – a toxic style of arguing – but I'm now aware of that. I knew I needed to change, to stop, and I did.

Music therapy

Anyway, back to the song with Betsy . . . My ex stormed out of the house after he'd lost it and left me cleaning up the mess. Once he was gone, Betsy looked away from the TV, at me, and said, 'I'll help you clean it, Mummy.' She went and fetched the dustpan and brush from under the sink, and began scooping up the Rice Krispies which had covered the entirety of the kitchen floor. I felt my heart shatter into a million more pieces. After 'Operation Clean-up', I gave the dog a treat, and I gave the rabbit a bowl of food so he would stay outside where he was safe and hidden in case my ex hadn't calmed down when he returned. Then I got Betsy in the car, and we went to soft play. It's amazing when I think back to how normal our lives must have seemed to the outside world, when all the while we were living in a war zone. As we were driving along, the Alesha Dixon song came on. We listened to the lyrics. It was really catchy and talked about the boy who never washes up or cleans anything.

Betsy said, 'This is a song about Daddy.'

It made me laugh out loud and my heart hurt all at the same time. After that day, it became our song. It was a secret, between her and me, and she knew that. Even at the tender age of four, she'd already learned the rules. After that, when he smashed something in rage and left the house, we would clean together while playing this song at full blast. We would dance, sing, clean and have fun. Yep, fun – during a time that was so fucking sick and wrong. Still, it somehow felt better than what had been happening in the years before that, when I would clean alone, in silence, or with a kids' TV show playing in the background, broken, with tears streaming down my face that I tried to hide from her.

We always played the song in the car together when things were bad; it was like therapy for us. We knew every word, line by line, and we would shout it together, attempting to let go of all the gross feelings we felt while being trapped by him. Sometimes, when she got bigger, and things were really bad at home, when he was really losing his temper, she would play the song in front of me.

Of course, it meant nothing to him, but to us it meant something, and I'd hear the lyrics amongst the chaos of him doing what he did best, and I'd look over at her, and she would look back at me, and we understood each other. Together. A secret from him but about him, which reminded me that no matter what he said, it was me and her against the world. It always would be.

After I left him, we kept playing the song together, usually on the way to school after she had spent a weekend with him, and she would angrily shout the lyrics. I recognised everything she was feeling as I watched her sing out her broken heart. It reminded me that although I had left, she was very much still living in a warzone. Sometimes she would call me from his house when she was with him, and if the song was on in the background, I knew she was letting me know things weren't great (although whenever I asked if she wanted me to collect her, her answer was always no). I knew how she was feeling, and the helplessness I felt at her situation haunted me daily.

Find your song
We all need to find our own song. We need to find the tune that lifts us and spurs us on, that feels like it was written for us, that we can share with others to help them feel their feelings too. Do you have a song, a heartbreak anthem? If not, find one. Music really is therapy – never underestimate the power of a dance or car karaoke.

When Betsy turned into a teenager, she stopped seeing her dad. I remember the day she made the decision never to see him again. I knew she was done, because I'd also been there, and I knew how much effort, time and love she'd put into trying to be a part of his world by that point. We got into my car, and she played the song. At the loudest volume possible.

We'd played it about a week earlier too, after an incident where he had lost his temper with her because she'd dropped one of her school shoes in the road when he collected her from me. She hadn't realised she'd dropped it until they got back to his house. When she told him, he lost it – to her face, and with me over the phone. I remember walking out of our home and seeing one lonely black Vans trainer lying next to the kerb. I picked it up and said to it, 'How have you caused so much destruction just by being here?' That day when she came home, we'd played Alesha's song, and it had felt sad because Betsy was still trapped by him. But this day, just a week later, on the day she made her choice to walk away from him, the song felt different. For the first time ever, it felt good and there was no sadness attached it. It was an achievement; it felt like our freedom song. *Our* song. A song that only we two would ever understand; a song that told the story of domestic abuse at its worse, and how we had escaped it.

When we played it on the way back from our podcast, we sang our hearts out and remembered every word. There

The power of music:
it's honestly like
nothing else.

was no shouting the lyrics with our eyes full of tears; there was no swallowing away those painful lumps in our throats after each chorus. There was no anger at our situation. There was just the two of us, giving it beans in the car, smiling and giggling as we sang, giving each other that look we began giving each other during the worst times of our lives, but that now meant something different. Now that look means *we did it*. It means we're free. It means we made it, along with her baby sister, who has absolutely no idea this song even exists. I imagine she will read this chapter and think, 'What the hell?'

The power of music: it's honestly like nothing else. If you're ever at my funeral or Betsy's, now you'll know the meaning of this song when it comes on. Because yes, of course, we've made that decision: it's being played at both.

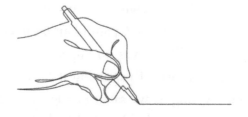

A note on sex and self-worth

When I met the girls' dad, my self-worth was on the floor. I don't remember when or how it got that low – perhaps it had been like that since the day my mum left – but I know one side effect of it was that I had zero respect for my own body. I would have sex, often unprotected, just to feel wanted. That was so fucked up, looking back, because more often than not, I *knew* the person having sex with me didn't really want me. I was just the girl available to them, the girl who was easy to take.

The other thing I find odd is that some of those boys and men had the ugliest personalities *and* appearances, yet still I allowed them to take full advantage of me. It's like I wanted to feel as shit and used as humanly possible, because that was what I thought I deserved. I'd have sex with them at their houses, in their cars, in public, wherever. Then I'd go home and just swipe another highlighter mark on another day in my diary, and be reminded of

Now I am the mum
of teens, I have a
huge responsibility
to ensure my
children know
their worth.

those feelings every time I sat and trawled through them, reminding myself what an awful human I was.

Now I am the mum of teens, I have a huge responsibility to ensure my children know their worth, and that they understand the mental and physical effects of unsafe, non-consensual or unprotected sex. My parents didn't do that for me, and I felt it. Sex cannot be hidden or pushed into dark corners of shame. It needs to be discussed openly. Other than one weird half-day sex education lesson at secondary school, there wasn't one adult who ever sat down and explained sex to me: what it meant; that I had a choice; that if I didn't do it responsibly, I could fuck up my entire life. Those highlighted swipes throughout five years' worth of teenage diaries were never a reflection of me being a terrible person, or a slut or a slag. They were a reflection of the lack of love I had around me from the adults who should have been there to care for me and show me that marking as many pages as I could with a highlighter pen wasn't an achievement, but nor was it anything to feel shame about. Those pen marks literally highlight the fact that if the adults around me had done the job they should have been committed to doing, then me having unsafe sex in an alley with someone who didn't care for me never would have happened.

Today, as the director of a women's centre I opened in 2021 to support little girls and mums going through the abuse I once went through, I work with teenage girls who are – in their own ways – swiping pages in a diary with highlighter pen far too often. We try to show them how incredible they are, even when they can't see it or refuse to believe it. We deliver a course each week to help them understand the effects of domestic abuse and learn how to look out for red flags in future relationships. I have worked with a hypnotherapist to create a trauma workshop to help these women and teenage girls make sense of things they feel shame and embarrassment about. I hope that, at the very least, our centre shows them that they are needed, that they are wanted, and that their value amounts to much more than the number of sexual encounters they've noted in their diary.

Afterword: Getting excited for the future

Our plan, right now, which we decided upon very recently, is to find a dream destination and secondary school, and leave Torbay in the year Wilby transitions from primary to secondary school. By that point, all his older siblings will have finished school, and all the kids bar Edie and Wilby will be adults. And so, we'll go. We'll leave this place, which feels unsafe to us, and is still full of jealous and bitter people that hate what and who we are, and we'll start afresh. I hope the kids will come along, but by that point, the big four will all be in their twenties and thirties, so who knows what life will look like for them then.

I'm excited for tomorrow, for next week, next year and forever.

I hope you are, too.

I'm happy, I'm content, and no matter what's going on in my life, every single day I am bubbling with gratitude for the life I have, and the life I've lived, even on the bad days.

I hope you have things in your life that make you happy and content; things that fill you with gratitude.

If you've got this far, thank you – whether you bought a signed copy of this book or found it covered in dust on a bookshelf on your holiday. I wouldn't be me without you. Nothing I have achieved would be possible without the backing of this kind, funny and incredible group of people I've met, both virtually or in person. Whether I chat to you all the time in my inbox, or you're one of my silent followers, just know I'm grateful to all of you every day.

I'm going to leave you with one last letter. I wrote it to me, from me (and maybe to you too!). But before I do, please note the following ideas and live by them:

- ♥ Take care of yourself and stay safe.
- ♥ Trust your gut and know your worth.
- ♥ Know you have the power in you to live and love how you want to.
- ♥ Remember there is more good than bad in the world, no matter how it feels sometimes. Look for the good – it's out there.
- ♥ Never forget that everything is temporary. This life we get is short and, as we see constantly, tomorrow isn't promised to any of us. So make the most of every day and meet people without judgement and with kindness.

A letter to myself, aged forty-one (1 January 2024)

Dear Rach,

Well, here it is, the 'Shit, I did it' letter I promised I'd be writing you all those years ago. We made it, you know. We're finally here. For so many years, you've lived with the worst imposter syndrome, and you've down-played your achievements and your wins – for many reasons.

The biggest one is because of your worry about the wankers on the internet, who sit behind their fake accounts, coming for you whenever something good happens in your life, or whenever you're happy. But as time's gone on (and they began their hate campaign back in 2019), the whole world has come to realise that what they do isn't personal. If you disappeared tomorrow, the trolls would forget you and move on to their next target. You see other people every day getting the same level of abuse and harassment, and it's become a little boring to everyone now. Irrelevant, actually.

The second reason is because, until the last few years, nothing has ever gone right for you – not for long periods, anyway, not consecutively. The thought of sharing the good stuff you've done leaves you with an overriding fear that doing so will somehow make it all go wrong.

The last reason is because we have this thing in our country where, when people share their successes, everyone judges them for being a narcissistic show-off or dickhead.

The reality is, when you achieve something good as a human – whether that's getting out of bed, brushing your teeth and showering, then going back to bed, googling a therapist to address your trauma, applying for that job promotion, or joining that gym – it should be celebrated. We should acknowledge the power we've found within us. Celebrating our wins, no matter how big or small, is something we should do all more of. It makes those who love us happy. And those who aren't excited to celebrate our victories? Well, that's nothing to do with you; it's none of your business. Remember that when comments from other people get under your skin.

So, Rach, let's celebrate what you achieved in 2023. The people surrounding you have started to feel safer again. And you started going to the gym, stuck at it, and actually began to love it. You learned fitness isn't about losing weight and cellulite – it's about loving your body for all it can do and has done. And it was the year you bought a campervan and sat under the stars, talking about everything and nothing, with the people you love – and you realised, for the first time in your life, what a natural high being out in nature gives you. And you worked your arse off, like you have the last few years, but for the first time ever, you started seeing the results. You finally began to notice the hard work paying off, and at times it's been a beautiful sight. It was a bittersweet year, too, because you noticed how quickly your babies are growing and how fast the people you love, yourself included, are ageing . . .

But 2024 has begun today! Let's look ahead. Let's write down our goals:

- You'll still work hard this year, but that's OK, because working hard when you're doing the stuff you love really is a dream, and the people you get to work alongside make it feel incredible every day.
- As well as working, you're going to travel and get in that campervan at every given opportunity.
- Share some of your life online, but not all of it. You've started to realise it's special when you do things just for you. And the people who love you? They want you to do that too.
- Make more plans, and try not to cancel.
- Keep walking to the beach late at night in stormy weather to watch the waves. The sea has always intrigued you and made you feel so many things – do more of that.
- Go for dinner with your friends.
- Go for lunch with your friends.
- Take your mother-in-law out for breakfast more, and ask her more questions. She loves to tell you her stories.
- Take your babies out, even if it's just for a night-time drive to get a milkshake together. Make memories

with them that will last a lifetime. They're growing so quickly, and there are no guarantees on how long they'll stick around, so while they're here, be present when you're in their company. Listen to them when they need you, because I promise, you won't feel like the supermarket deli counter forever – and one day you'll wish you still did.

💜 Buy more stuff for the campervan: more board games, more fairy lights, more blankets, more jigsaw puzzles. This is your safe place and second home – prioritise keeping it feeling like that, and forever play draughts with your husband into the night. These are the glimmers. These are the in-the-moment moments we all need to treasure.

💜 Compliment people. When someone looks good, smells good, achieves something, don't be afraid to stop and tell them.

💜 Keep going to the gym, no matter how much you can't be arsed some days. Remind yourself how much stronger your body and mind have felt since starting, and how much you enjoy the feel-good endorphin rush that you feel post-workout.

💜 Lastly, and maybe most importantly, look out for the powerful magic in the people around you, and the powerful magic within yourself. Remember how many times over the years you've doubted yourself, then think back to the day you were moved down a set in English at school when you were fourteen because you weren't performing, and Mrs King said, 'It pains me to do this, because you are one of the most incredible writers I have ever come across, and my only wish for you would be that you see that in yourself and put the effort in; it could really take you places.' Point out people's magic to them. Make them see it, believe in it – it could change their lives.

Be you, unapologetically you – the sweary, chaotic, emotional, vulnerable, disorganised you – because, for the first time in your life, you're starting to like yourself – and it's a fucking incredible place to be.

I love you. I'm proud of you.

Rach xx

PS Never doubt how much you deserve this! Four-year-old Rach is buzzing that we made it.

Acknowledgements

For Winston, our beautiful boy who passed away just after I handed in my first manuscript.

Many people understand the pain of losing a dog but I didn't until you left us. You going knocked us like nothing we've ever felt before. The pain of saying goodbye absolutely floored us. What it also did, though, was show me how close we are as a family. It taught us all we need to be together in times of need. We had to unite to heal, together, through love alone and I believe you left us that insight – your final gift – to show us how incredible we are as a family unit.

Thank you for loving us for your whole life; every single day without question.

Hope you're eating chicken nuggets every day buddy, beach walks aren't the same without your craziness.

We miss you and we love you more than you could have ever known.